The SECRETS of CONSULTING

A GUIDE TO GIVING & GETTING ADVICE SUCCESSFULLY

The SECRETS of CONSULTING

A GUIDE TO GIVING & GETTING ADVICE SUCCESSFULLY

GERALD M. WEINBERG

FOREWORD BY VIRGINIA SATIR

Dorset House Publishing
353 West 12th Street
New York, N.Y. 10014

Library of Congress Cataloging in Publication Data

Weinberg, Gerald M.
   The secrets of consulting.

   Bibliography: p.
   Includes index.
   1. Consultants.   I. Title.
HD69.C6W45   1985   658.4'6   85-72964
ISBN 0-932633-01-3 (pbk.)

Illustrator: Joseph Peragine
Cover: Margot Schwaab

Printed in the United States of America

Library of Congress Catalog Number 85-72964

ISBN: 0-932633-01-3

Preface

If you are a consultant, or if you ever use a consultant, this book is for you. That's a wide scope, because nowadays, nearly everyone is some kind of a consultant. There are hardware consultants and software consultants, social workers and psychiatrists, management consultants and worker consultants, energy consultants and information consultants, safety consultants and accident consultants, beauty consultants and septic tank consultants, consulting physicians and consulting attorneys, wedding consultants, decorators, genetic consultants, family therapists, economic consultants, bankruptcy consultants, retirement consultants, funeral consultants, and psychic consultants.

And those are only the professionals. You're using a consultant when you ask your neighbor what he uses to remove crabgrass from his lawn. You're being a consultant when your daughter asks you what college she ought to attend. In the United States, at least, you don't have to have a license to advise someone on what car to buy, or to help another find the quickest route to Arkadelphia.

With such diversity, what do all these consultants have in common? What would make them all want to read this book? My definition of consulting is *the art of influencing people at their request*. People want some sort of change—or fear some sort of change—so they seek consulting, in one form or another.

Many people influence other people without a request. A judge can sentence you to thirty years of hard labor. Your teacher can assign you thirty pages of hard reading. Your boss can give you thirty days of hard traveling. Your priest can apportion you thirty Hail Marys. Judges and teachers and bosses and priests *can* act as consultants. But they're not consultants in these cases, because these forms of influence are enforced by some authority system, not necessarily by the willing participation of the person influenced.

Other influencers have no authority, but are not consultants because they lack the request. Car dealers and other salespeople come to mind in this category. Again, they *may* act as consultants, but they're not consultants when they're trying to sell you something you didn't ask for.

Being *called* a consultant doesn't make you a consultant, either. Many people are called consultants as a way of glorifying their dull jobs. Some "software consultants," for instance, are retained strictly as supplementary programming labor. The last thing their "clients" want is to be influenced. All they want is grunt work turning out computer code, but by calling their temporary workers "consultants," they can get them for a few dollars less than if they called them something more mundane.

Conversely, you may be a consultant even if you don't have the label. Anyone with a staff job is acting as a consultant to the line management. When they hired you, they were requesting your influence (why else would someone hire a staff person?). After you've been on the payroll for a while, however, they may forget that you were hired to help. Sometimes, even *you* forget, so your task is a bit different from that of the outsider called in to work on a specific problem.

This is not a book about how to become a consultant. That part is easy. Most likely, you already *are* a consultant, because you become a consultant whenever you accept someone's request for influence. It's *after* you accept the request that you start needing help. When I became a full-time consultant, I soon discovered that few people request influence when their world is behaving rationally. As a result, consultants tend to see more than their fair share of irrationality. You may have noticed, for instance, how frequently someone who asks you for advice will then attack you angrily because of the requested advice. Such irrationality drives consultants crazy, but if they can cope with it, it can also drive them rich.

There were times, though, when I couldn't cope with it, so I turned to writing books to restore my sanity. Anyone who is irrational enough to buy one of my books may be requesting influence, but at least I don't have to give the advice face-to-face. That's why my books are cheaper than my consulting fees.

Most of the time, though, I enjoyed the direct interaction with my clients, if I could stand the irrationality. If I wanted to stay in the business, it seemed to me I had two choices:

1.   Remain rational, and go crazy.

2.   Become irrational, and be called crazy.

For many years, I oscillated between these poles of misery, until I hit upon a third approach:

3.   Become rational about irrationality.

This book relates some of my discoveries about the rationality of seemingly irrational behavior that surrounds requests for influence. These are the secrets of consulting. The title suggests that this is a book for consultants, but the book is actually for anyone who is confused by our irrational world and would like to do something about it. That's an almost limitless audience.

Even if you're so confused that nobody calls upon you for consulting, perhaps you need a consultant yourself. You might just save the cost of a consultant by reading this book. Or get more mileage out of the fees you pay your consultants.

But if you're *not* confused, you definitely don't need this book. You need a psychiatrist. Anyone who's not confused in today's world has to be out of touch with reality.

What will reading the book do for you? Many people have read the manuscript, and some of them claim to have been influenced in positive ways. One consultant says she applied one of the laws, called The Orange Juice Test, and obtained a fat contract that she would probably have otherwise lost. Another said he negotiated a larger fee by applying The Principle of Least Regret. A third lost a fat contract by applying the same Principle, but he didn't mind very much, which is why it's called The Principle of Least Regret. One manager told me that as soon as he finished reading the manuscript, he fired a consultant who had been costing him three thousand dollars a month. He didn't say whether the consultant had any regrets.

Not all of the influence has been directly financial. Several readers say that they enjoy their consulting more, now that they understand a bit more about what's going on. One staff product director told me he applied his new knowledge of buffalo and dogs to get a higher percentage of his recommendations implemented by his marketing manager. Another staffer could give no specific examples except to say that her boss complimented her for "thinking better."

One old-time consultant told me a long-winded story about how he used to spend a lot of time worrying about the fact that he didn't have a Ph.D. (I think he was getting his revenge for some of my long-winded stories in the book.) He had taken several years out of his life to go back to school for his doctorate, only to discover that his clients weren't interested in degrees. "Reading the book was like going for my Ph.D. I didn't really need to read it, but if I hadn't read it, I would have thought I needed to read it." As you'll learn in the very first chapter, that's the best result any consultant can hope to achieve.

August 1985   G.M.W.
Lincoln, Nebraska

Foreword

Reading *The Secrets of Consulting* is a very special experience. The book appeals to my sense of humor, my awareness of human foibles, and my knowledge of how human systems work. Most especially, this book enlarges my view of how change takes place, of how a consultant in any context can become more effective.

It is profound in its meaning and humorous and colorful in its presentation. Jerry Weinberg's style is such that he shares his experiences and knowledge with me; I feel inspired, rather than defensive. As I read, I can identify with the people and the problems he describes, and I take pleasure in laughing at myself and in learning from the situations that apply to me.

The Secrets of Consulting is far more than a consultant's handbook. It is actually a book about how people can take charge of their own growth. As a family therapist, I've found it helpful to understand people's behavior and the relationship between consultant and client by relating it to our birth into this world, an appearance into an unequal triad: father, mother, child. The father and mother are supposedly grown, and the child is totally dependent on the adults. What we learn from birth to adulthood is related essentially to this; although much of what we learn is unconscious, it gives us both our feelings about ourselves and about our importance to the world. It also gives us skills for coping, which can be augmented by consultants.

Unconscious or not, our basic childhood learnings still operate, whether we're in the role of client or consultant. Jerry Weinberg often gently teases the reader, as well as himself, about some of these powerful unconscious lessons that get in the way of our hoped-for results. For example, every one of us needs approval and open recognition of success: "Look, Ma, no hands," says the proud son while riding his bicycle, hoping Mama will smile. When Mama doesn't, the child's need is unfulfilled and, as an adult, he may still look for that smile, but in the wrong context.

Further, many of us still dance between the wish and need to know and the fear of rejection that might come from revealing our needs. "After all," we think to ourselves, "If I am smart, I should know everything already and be able to handle every situation well. If I don't, it is a sign of my weakness, stupidity, perverseness, or incompetence. Acknowledging such flaws would be intolerable." When this interpretation is made, most of us play games, either hiding our true feelings or projecting them onto someone else: thinking, for example, "I don't need you. And if it looks as if I do, it is probably because *you* are at fault."

Giving help, offering new ways to cope, is the consultant's job; but in order for the consultant to succeed, the job needs to be framed and approached with just that dance in mind. By asking for the consultant's help, the client is saying, sometimes nonverbally, "I need you. I can't say so directly, so find a way to help me without destroying my sense of worth." The wise consultant answers in a way that recognizes the client's self-worth, but also doesn't compromise his own. Otherwise, no real or lasting change can take place.

As the wise consultant, Jerry Weinberg illustrates this key point in many different contexts. He points to effective and interesting ways to approach the dance, and always praises the client who knows when and whom to ask for help as a mark of greater intelligence than as an admission of incompetence. In this context, both client and consultant grow in learning and strength, and everyone feels good.

After all, aren't the secrets of consulting basically what growth, competence, and good human relations are about? Namely, that we feel good about ourselves and about others, and that we experience our hopes and goals being fulfilled.

October 1985   Virginia Satir
Palo Alto, California   Director of Training
                                                      Avanta Network

Contents

The **SECRETS** of CONSULTING

A GUIDE TO GIVING & GETTING ADVICE SUCCESSFULLY

1

why consulting is so tough

The wider you spread it, the thinner it gets.
—The Law of Raspberry Jam

Have you ever dreamed of owning a restaurant? of concocting delicious meals for appreciative customers and ending each evening by counting the thousands of dollars piled up in the cash register? Recently, I found a book on starting your own restaurant. I was dying to read all about the glamour, the independence, and the riches, but the author wasted the entire first chapter trying to talk me out of my dream. "Put down this book," he urged, "and find yourself a sensible trade."

But I was not so easily dissuaded, not after a lifetime of dreams. I went on to the other chapters, only to find them full of questions to warn me about the ugly realities of the restaurant world: How will you fight off creditors, extortionists, and all your friends who want free meals? How do you deal with an invasion of cockroaches the day before the health inspector arrives? with disgustingly spoiled food when the refrigerator breaks down? with waiters who quit in the middle of your busiest night? What do you do when customers simply don't come through the door? What do you do when they *do* come? get loudly drunk? vomit all over the floor?

Eventually, he convinced me. Sadder but wiser, I put aside my restaurant fantasies and returned to the mundane task of being a consultant.

Have *you* ever dreamed of becoming a consultant? traveling on an expense account to glamorous places? giving brilliant advice to eager clients who follow it immediately and without question? raking in enormous fees with a minimum of work?

For those of us who would escape our miserable lot in life, consultant fantasies run a close second to restaurant fantasies. So before we get too far into the other secrets of consulting, we'd better face The Number One Secret:

Consulting ain't as easy as it looks.

In this chapter, we'll see some of the reasons why.

SHERBY'S LAWS OF CONSULTING

It's difficult for an executive to criticize a budget when most line items are for mysterious high technology activities. It's easier to tackle the more understandable portions, like postage, janitorial services, and consulting.

Executives may not understand microprogramming or micro-economics, but they understand consulting. I've never met an executive who didn't have a favorite—unflattering—joke about consultants. But, then, I've never met a consultant who didn't have a worse joke about executives.

In any high technology area of business, consultants' fees will be a substantial budget item, but the antagonism between managers and consultants often wastes most of this money. The manager who under-stands this antagonism will get more value out of the consulting budget. That's why I often speak to management and consultant groups about their relationship.

Even so, I rarely speak to both managers and consultants in the same audience; the first time I did, I almost created a riot. The audience had just finished a rather large steak preceded by a rather long cocktail hour, so before starting the serious part of my speech, I told a joke to get their attention:

> On the first day of spring, Zeke and Luke decided to go bear hunting. It was too late to hunt when they reached their cabin, so they spent the first evening reducing their beer inventory. Just before dawn, Luke awoke and went out into the woods to answer the call of nature. Unfortunately, on his way back, he crossed the path of a huge grizzly bear out looking for breakfast. The bear started for Luke, and Luke started for the cabin. Just as the bear was about to grab Luke by the neck, Luke tripped and fell flat on his face. The bear, which was going too fast to stop, ran right past Luke and through the open cabin door. Thinking quickly, Luke jumped up, slammed and latched the door, and called into his sleep-ing partner, "You skin that one, Zeke, while I go fetch another."

The joke was well received, but some well-oiled manager called out, "That's just like a consultant. They always bring up grizzly prob-lems and then leave us managers to solve them."

At that, an angry consultant jumped to his feet and said, "You've got it backwards. *Luke* was the manager. Managers handle all the easy problems themselves, but when they get something they can't handle, they lock it in the cabin with the consultant."

From there, I lost control of the audience, and nobody even noticed when I left the podium and fetched a second dessert. As I spooned in the melted rainbow sherbet, I tried to think of some way to stop the argument and help managers and consultants to understand each other.

Perhaps it was the sherbet, but what popped into my mind were three laws my friend Roger House had told me, under the title of Sherby's Laws of Consulting. I never met Sherby, but I like laws. I especially like irrational-sounding laws that can be used to capture the attention of an unruly audience. I coughed into the microphone, tried to look as much like Moses as possible, and pronounced, "We consultants have three ironclad laws. Ordinarily, we don't speak of these laws to our clients, but I think that it will help if I reveal them to the managers here."

The promise of some trade secrets brought the audience back under control, so I continued. "Here are the three laws, which all consultants must remember when taking on a new assignment." I enunciated them slowly, writing each one on the chalkboard:

The First Law of Consulting:
In spite of what your client may tell you, there's always a problem.

The Second Law of Consulting:
No matter how it looks at first, it's always a people problem.

The Third Law of Consulting:
Never forget they're paying you by the hour, not by the solution.

As I had hoped, the audience was completely puzzled, stopped in its tracks. I had everyone's full attention and could now continue my speech on the client-consultant relationship.

There's Always a Problem

Nothing is more puzzling to a young consultant than to arrive at the client's office and be told, first thing, "We really don't have any problems here. Nothing that we can't handle, anyway."

Indeed, more than one green consultant has been so ignorant as to reply, "If there is no problem, then why did you hire me?" This may seem logical, but logic and culture have nothing to do with one another. In the culture of management, the worst thing you can do is admit to anyone that you have a problem you can't handle by yourself. If you really do need help, you have to sneak it in somehow without admitting in public that there is any problem at all.

The Ten Percent Promise

There's no curing sick people who believe they are well, but The First Law of Consulting says that they'll never admit that they are sick.

So consultants have a big problem. One way around the problem is to agree that the client is competent, and then ask if there are any areas that need improvement. Few people are willing to admit that they're sick, but most of us are willing to admit that we could use improvement. Unless we're *really* sick.

But be careful not to overdo this ploy out of eagerness to get the job. If you promise too much improvement, they'll never hire you, because that would force them to admit they had a problem. A corollary of The First Law of Consulting is The Ten Percent Promise Law:

Never promise more than ten percent improvement.

Most people can successfully absorb ten percent into their psychological category of "no problem." Anything more, however, would be embarrassing if the consultant succeeded.

The Ten Percent Solution

Another corollary is The Ten Percent Solution Law:

If you happen to achieve more than ten percent improvement, make sure it isn't noticed.

The best way to make sure it isn't noticed, of course, is to help the client take all the credit. Consultants who don't bury their huge successes are like guests who clean their shoes on the table napkins. They aren't invited back.

It's Always a People Problem

One way for managers to avoid mentioning that they have a problem is to label the problem a "technical problem." Technical problems aren't really supposed to be a manager's responsibility. Besides, in a high technology business, it wouldn't be possible to keep all the expertise you need on the payroll.

When reviewing budgets, executives should allow their managers to save face by hiding management consulting under a cloak of technical consulting. Everyone needs outside help from time to time, so why embarrass anyone?

Even when it's "really" a technical problem, it can always be traced back to management action or inaction. Even so, the experienced consultant will resist pointing out that it was management who hired all the technical people and is responsible for their development. At the same time, the consultant will look for the people who should have prevented this problem, or dealt with it when it arose.

Marvin's Law

A corollary of The Second Law of Consulting is one of Marvin's Laws:

Whatever the client is doing, advise something else.

At the very least, the people problem is either lack of imagination or lack of perspective. People who are close to a problem tend to keep repeating what didn't work the first time. If it did work, they wouldn't have called in a consultant. Since every hard-working person loses perspective at times, executives should be wary of managers who *never* call in outside consultants. They are so close to their problems that they don't know how much trouble they're in.

Never Forget They're Paying You by the Hour

The Third Law of Consulting *could* be interpreted to mean that the consultant should milk the client for as much hourly money as possible, but that's not what it's about. Many good consultants have tried to get paid by the solution, but none to my knowledge has ever succeeded. To succeed, you would first have to get the client to admit that there was a problem, then that the problem was big enough to justify paying you well for solving it.

The Third Law of Consulting actually reminds the consultant that if the clients had *wanted* a solution, they would have *paid* for a solution. Deep down, people want to be able to say to their management, "Look, we realize that there is a problem, and we are working on it. We have retained a consultant."

Later, when the consultant leaves, the statement is changed to, "How could we be expected to solve this problem? We had a high-priced consultant here for three months, and she couldn't solve it. It obviously just can't be solved."

The Credit Rule

In short, managers may not be buying solutions, but alibis to give *their* management. A corollary of The Third Law of Consulting is The Credit Rule:

You'll never accomplish anything if you care who gets the credit.

In order for a consultant to get credit, the client would have to admit there had been a solution. To admit there was a solution, the client would have to admit there was a problem, which is unthinkable. As a result, the only consultants who get invited back are those who never seem to accomplish anything.

Whether these consultants actually do accomplish anything is an unanswerable question. Whichever way it was answered, it would leave the consultant out of a job, so effective consultants make sure it is never asked. Unfortunately, so do ineffective consultants. The difference, however, is that when an effective consultant is present, the *client* solves problems.

The Lone Ranger Fantasy

It's hard to work without taking credit, especially because our unfulfilled desires can interfere with our performance as consultants. One particular consultant reacted to Sherby's Laws and their corollaries by saying, "They're not as applicable to computer consulting, where most clients really are paying for a solution, and where admitting confusion about computers is almost a badge of honor among executives." Out of a need to feel that she's accomplishing something, this consultant may overlook a possible consulting opportunity: Working with these executives, she might create a situation in which they'll take personal responsibility as the managers who created the technical organization that's not effective at solving its own problems.

Contrast this consultant with another one who wrote, "I always try to give teachers alternative strategies to use on a child's problem, and I always give public credit to the teachers for successful remediation of the child's need. I always try to teach them techniques so they won't have to call me back for the same problem the next time. But I have my own needs to take care of, so I concocted The Lone Ranger Fantasy. As I exit from the case, I visualize myself galloping off into the sunset while the teachers shake their heads and say, 'Who was that masked woman, anyway?'"

I use the same fantasy myself, and so do many older consultants who grew up in the golden days of radio. Younger consultants who don't know the Lone Ranger so intimately might think of The Lone Ranger Fantasy this way:

When the clients don't show their appreciation, pretend that they're stunned by your performance—but never forget that it's your fantasy, not theirs.

The Fourth Law of Consulting

In organizational consulting, Sherby's Laws of Consulting expose the essential competition between managers and consultants. Both managers and consultants are paid for their ability to solve problems. For either to admit the need for the other would be an admission of their own inadequacy. Only the best managers and consultants are big enough to admit that they can't do it all by themselves. Even managers sometimes need The Lone Ranger Fantasy.

The same contradiction applies to anyone who calls upon a consultant. Indeed, you could define "consultant" as "someone who helps you solve problems you think you should be able to solve by yourself." Therefore, hiring a consultant is always seen as an admission of personal failure. A consultant who fails to solve the problem would thus be interpreted as a personal success for the client—except that the client hired the consultant in the first place, and so the consultant's failure still falls on the client.

People who weren't involved in the hiring decision have no such restraints. They will always be delighted when the consultant fails to solve their problem. Which leads to my final law, which I'll add to Sherby's:

If they didn't hire you, don't solve their problem.

The Fourth Law of Consulting says you must never allow yourself to forget that consulting is the art of influencing people *at their request*. Among consultants, the most prevalent occupational disease is offering unsolicited "help." It's bad for your bankbook, and it doesn't work. In fact, it usually backfires.

THE LAW OF RASPBERRY JAM

I learned to pay attention to The Fourth Law of Consulting because, as a kid, I had two clear goals. I wanted to help other people, and I wanted to get rich doing it. Throughout my life, I've struggled to achieve a balance between those two contradictory goals.

One of my first jobs was dishwashing—a good way to change a dirty world into a cleaner world. I've always enjoyed dishwashing jobs. Although the pay wasn't outstanding, there was always the sense of accomplishment when, in the end, I would triumph over some sticky raspberry jam. Not so, unfortunately, in my other attempts to change the world, as consultant, trainer, lecturer, and author. There, The Law of Raspberry Jam has been my unrelenting nemesis.

Washing dishes provides a satisfying, intimate relationship with the object of my work. Whatever my hands do is reflected immediately in a clean fork, a broken saucer, a sparkling goblet. If my son discovers peanut butter encrusted in the handle of a coffee mug, I take full blame. If my mother-in-law admires her face in the gleaming bottom of a frying pan, I take full credit. Although I suffer from the defeats, I learn to achieve more victories, and that's the essence of job satisfaction.

As a dishwashing *consultant,* I lose this immediate satisfaction. If my client is having problems with encrusted peanut butter, I can render advice or even demonstrate improved technique. But in spite of my best efforts, the peanut butter may remain encrusted, because it's up to my client to implement the ideas.

As compensation for losing the intimacy of dishwashing, the consultant gains the satisfaction of a much wider effect on the world's gunk, grease, and grime. In the time it would take to wash a hundred mugs, I can advise two other people on how to do the job in my absence. What I lose in quality, I gain in quantity.

As a dishwashing *trainer,* I intensify the quality/quantity tradeoff, because training is merely a cheaper form of consulting. Instead of giving one client my undivided attention, I design a workshop that can handle fifteen or twenty. Each participant gets a little less, but the cost goes down, so the market for my message expands. Sure, a couple will miss some essential point, and may leave *their* dishes actually grungier than before. But isn't it worth it to spread the word?

As a dishwashing *lecturer,* I can spread my consulting advice even further, reaching several hundred avid clients at one time. True, some of them may be sleeping with their eyes open, and a few might even think I said to rub peanut butter on, rather than off. But shouldn't I think of the greater good for the greater number?

But why stop there? Through the miracle of the printing press, I can reach *hundreds of thousands* of clients with my sterling advice. If my book on dishwashing is a bestseller, I might even reach millions! And earn millions!

Yes, what about the money? The going rate for dishwashers around here is about $9,000 a year. In contrast to that, a consultant might make $30,000; a trainer, $50,000; a lecturer, $80,000; and an author (better than me!), $150,000. In each case, the wider the audience, the more you can make.

The implications are obvious. Nobody ever gets rich washing dishes, no matter how much they enjoy the immediate gratification. And although consultants may live well, they don't retire early, the way lecturers and authors sometimes do. So keep your hands out of the dishwater and on the keyboard! You'll not only get rich, but you'll have a vast influence on the health and cleanliness of the nation!

Or so it would seem, but for that damnable Law of Raspberry Jam! And what is this ironclad principle standing between me and happy riches? Take a small jar of raspberry jam and a few loaves of bread. With a bit of experimentation, you will soon observe that

The wider you spread it, the thinner it gets.

Alas for those of us who would change the world and get rich doing it, The Law of Raspberry Jam is a true law of nature, as solid as the first law of thermodynamics. You could just as easily build a perpetual motion machine as you can make the jam both thicker and wider at the same time. Another way of expressing the law is this:

Influence or affluence; take your choice.

Every would-be helper must bow before The Law of Raspberry Jam. Shout through a megaphone or talk into a microphone. Train a disciple or create a church. Teach a class or build a university. None of these methods will thicken the message by so much as a single cubit.

WEINBERGS' LAW OF TWINS

As one of my experiments with The Law of Raspberry Jam, I wrote a book entitled *The Psychology of Computer Programming*. True to the law, the book did make me rich, in a modest way, but it wasn't very influential. After a dozen years, it was still selling well, which meant that the problems it described hadn't been solved. I know I shouldn't be ungrateful, but even so, I regret the title. Since its publication, clients keep accusing me of being a psychologist. Although many psychologists are consultants, and many consultants are psychologists, it's possible to be one without being the other. So let me set the record straight. I am not now, nor have I ever been, a psychologist. If you're depressed, don't write to me asking for a cure. If you can't resist picking items off K-Mart's shelves and dropping them into your bloomers, call someone else.

I have no certification as a psychologist. I have no degree in psychology. I was never initiated into the Secrets of Human Behavior, not even one tiny Secret of Human Behavior. In fact, when I went to college, I studiously *avoided* taking psychology courses, or even being seen with a psychology professor,

Until recently, I suspected that the entire field of psychology was fifty percent error and fifty percent fake. I further suspected that even the psychologists didn't know which half was which. As I matured, however, I began to respect the work of a select few psychologists, mostly those who could write plain English.

Being mistaken for a psychologist has helped me appreciate the psychologist's plight. If you're a nuclear physicist, gimleted bores don't pin you to the wall and offer their latest theory of strange quarks. But every bore and bartender is an expert in human behavior, without benefit of license, degree, course, training, or book.

Unfortunately for the certified psychologist, *most* of human behavior is ridiculously simple to predict. From the meteorologists, we learn that two-thirds of the time you can predict tomorrow's weather by saying it will be the same as today's. This makes everyone an expert on the weather—with only sixty-six percent accuracy. No wonder there are so many experts in psychology, where we can predict ninety-nine percent of human behavior with one simple law: Weinbergs' Law of Twins.

Even if you took a psychology course, your professors never would have taught you Weinbergs' Law of Twins. You must not blame them, nor sue for a tuition refund. Nobody wants to give away professional secrets. Would you take psychology courses if you knew that they covered only one percent of the subject, and that you could learn the other ninety-nine percent in one painless minute?

Like many of the truly great laws, this one had the most humble of beginnings. My wife, Dani, and I were sitting on the M104 bus, heading up New York's Broadway in the gloom of a winter rush hour. A haggard but pretty young woman boarded with eight children in tow. "How much is the fare?" she asked the driver.

"Thirty-five cents for adults, and children five and under ride free."

"Okay," she said, shifting one of the two tiniest under her arm so she could reach her purse. Dropping two coins in the meter, she started to parade her entourage down the aisle.

"Hey, wait a minute, lady!" the driver commanded, as only a New York City bus driver can. "You don't expect me to believe that all eight of them children is under six!"

"Of course, they are," she said indignantly. "These two are four, the two girls are three, both toddlers are two, and these little ones are one."

The driver was dumbfounded, and apologetic. "Gee, lady, I'm sorry. Do you *always* have twins?"

"Heavens, no," she said, managing to straighten a wisp of brown hair. "Most of the time we don't have *any*."

Whammo! Dani looked at me. I looked at Dani. Like the other passengers, we were amused at the miscommunication, but something bigger had flashed upon both of us at once.

We had just come from a frustrating consulting job, where nothing we did seemed to change anything. We couldn't figure out why we weren't successful, but as we thought of this poor couple doing what poor couples do and *most* of the time not making *any* babies, let alone twins, we had the insight we'd been seeking:

Most of the time, for most of the world, no matter how hard people work at it, nothing of any significance happens.

You can test this idea. Look around you, then close your eyes for one minute. When you open your eyes, most of the time you'll see almost exactly the same thing. In other words, for most systems in the world, the best prediction about their behavior in the *next* instant is just what they were doing in the *previous* instant.

We were elated! And why not. Here we had a law that applied equally well to planets and polymers, porcelains and peonies, parliaments and pajamas. And, best of all, to people!

Of course, for various reasons we didn't do anything about our great discovery. To do anything significant would have violated Weinbergs' Law itself. Oh, we had lots of good *reasons* for doing nothing, but reasons are merely *words*. The law says nothing about words, only about events. *Words* are easy to change, but don't accomplish much.

Why didn't Weinbergs' Law of Twins make us famous? It seems that most people claim that they already knew this law, although nobody ever gave us a reference to a publication in a respectable journal. But, then, everybody claims to be an expert in psychology.

Perhaps the problem is that people *expect* too much of a law, particularly if it's a *psychological* law. They want the law to tell them *how* to change, or even more important, how to change *other people*. But, to their disappointment, Weinbergs' Law tells them that most of their efforts will come to naught, even if they only want to change themselves.*

---

*Dani and I did eventually publish an entire book on the subject of *why* Weinbergs' Law prevails. It's called *On the Design of Stable Systems*, and if you want to buy a copy, we're sure John Wiley & Sons would be more than happy to oblige you. And we'll be more than happy to collect the royalties. It's a little heavier than this book, both in weight and treatment. You may even enjoy it, but if you think it will teach you how to change the world, you're doomed to disappointment. Long live The Law of Raspberry Jam!

RUDY'S RUTABAGA RULE

I'm not a complete pessimist. I'll admit that once in a while someone actually solves a problem. Sometimes, I even solve a problem myself. Like last night, when I noticed that the faucet was dripping and I wasn't able to sleep. I got up, tried to turn off the water, and found that the washer was worn through. I stumbled down to the basement, located my tools, retrieved a replacement washer, staggered back up the stairs, replaced the washer, and stopped the drip. I was quite pleased with myself.

People who become consultants probably had early experiences of actually solving a few problems. This tasty bait encourages them to try again, and a few lucky successes in a row sets the hook for life. My first job was delivering newspapers. I then advanced to soda jerk in a four-stool drug store. Thousands of scoops later, I worked my way up to six stools, then twelve. Each of these jobs presented me with a series of minor problems I could easily conquer.

My big break came at the age of thirteen when I got a job as a relief stock boy in Hillman's Supermarket. As relief stock boy, I got to work every department in the store when the regular stock boy had a day off. With this kind of job, I had lots of opportunity to learn the entire grocery business. Within a few weeks, I was familiar with the operation of most parts of the store. I started looking around for problems to solve.

I began to notice patterns. I noticed the counter behind the cigarette display where repentant shoppers hid jars of olives and bags of jelly beans. I also noticed that even though I put the oldest items in front, dated items in the dairy case were always taken in reverse order.

But mostly I noticed the rutabagas. I not only *noticed* the rutabagas, I made their acquaintance. I appreciated that each rutabaga had a distinct personality, and week after week I recognized the same rutabagas smiling at me from the same produce section. Evidently, nobody ever *bought* rutabagas. Rutabagas were just a permanent decoration, smiling their happy smiles at all the shoppers.

One morning, I was standing in the produce section with Rudy, the produce manager, trying to figure out how to place the fresh vegetables in the limited counter space. Rudy had wrestled with this problem for a long time but didn't seem to be getting anywhere. He asked if I had any bright ideas—and suddenly I was a consultant!

"I've noticed," I suggested, "that the rutabagas don't seem very popular. In fact, they seem to be the least popular vegetable we have in the store. Would it be any great loss if we didn't use *any* counter space for the rutabagas and used it maybe for something else?"

Rudy looked at me sideways. I knew I was in serious trouble for implying that a mere, temporary stock clerk could help him solve his problems. But he *had* asked for help. To my surprise, he suddenly smiled and grabbed an empty banana box. Sweeping the rutabagas into the box, he said, "That's a great idea, kid."

I beamed with a consultant's pride. For the first time in my life, an adult had actually listened to me and taken my advice. Rudy looked at the void left by the departed rutabagas, then looked at me, then at the many vegetables that still had to be stocked, then at me again. After a long pause, he said, "Well, kid, that was a great idea. *Now* what's the least popular vegetable?"

After Rutabagas, Then What?

I've had thousands of consulting clients since then, but I can still hear Rudy's scratchy voice asking that killer question. My great idea had a fatal flaw. I can remove one problem that's my worst, but it always leaves another that used to be my *second* worst.

Often when teaching a class, I've had some pain-in-the-neck student who was clearly my worst problem. If I induced this student to drop the class, for a moment I would think, "Now, I'm in great shape."

Yet almost before the thought was formed, another student would start causing trouble. This new pain-in-the-neck used to be my second worst problem but now that the first one was gone, he had ascended to the top of the list. Once in a great while, though, I do remember Rudy's Rutabaga Rule in time. Like last night, after I'd fixed the faucet.

I crawled back into bed thinking, "Now that the worst noise is stilled, I'll be able to sleep." For a few minutes, it was quiet. Then I heard a loose end of antenna wire flapping in the wind and tapping against a window. Stirred by my success with the washer, I could easily have gone out in the wintry cold with a two-story ladder, and tried to fix that wire. But Rudy's voice warned me it would just lead to the discovery of some other problem. That cursed wire flapped all night, and I didn't get any sleep at all. But I didn't fall off any ladder, either.

There's just no escaping Rudy's Rutabaga Rule:

Once you eliminate your number one problem, number two gets a promotion.

As a consultant, I often get so involved in my clients' problems, that I begin to believe I could actually rid them of problems once and for all. But, according to Rudy, there's *always* another problem.

THE HARD LAWS OF CONSULTING

At the beginning of this chapter, I promised that I would try to discourage you from entering the consulting business. First, I hit you with Sherby's Laws, which warned you that nobody really wants your help, and that even when people seem to be asking for it, they're really only fooling you.

Then, I revealed The Law of Raspberry Jam, which showed you the futility of trying to be an effective human being and make a decent living at the same time. But perhaps that only bothered you until you learned Weinbergs' Law of Twins, which made it quite clear that you weren't likely to be effective in any case.

But just on the chance that you happen to be effective, Rudy's Rutabaga Rule demonstrates that you'll merely bring up another problem to replace the one you've somehow managed to solve. And if by some remote fluke you solve the second one, there will be another. And another. And then another, ad infinitum.

When you opened this book, you were, in effect, asking me to be your consultant. You've read all these secrets, my finest consulting efforts. By this time you ought to have put down the book and renounced your foolish fantasies. But, according to The Law of Raspberry Jam, you probably haven't learned a thing.

Actually, if you want to be a consultant, and if you haven't put down this volume by now, it's probably a good sign: You don't give up easily. So now I'm going to reward you by letting you in on the real secrets of consulting: The Hard Law, The Harder Law, and The Hardest Law.

The Hard Law

We've seen how difficult change is. This difficulty suggests that most of your consulting interventions simply won't work. If that prospect sends you into deep depression, stay out of the consulting trade. But if you're already in the racket, you'd better learn to live with failure.

That's what I call The Hard Law:

If you can't accept failure, you'll never succeed as a consultant.

This is truly a hard law, yet expressed in inverse form, it offers an atom of hope:

Some people do succeed as consultants, so it must be possible to deal with failure.

So what keeps successful consultants going, even when they fail?

The Harder Law

Why is there always another problem? It seems to me that people *need* to solve problems—and we consultants are the neediest of the lot. For us, solving problems is synonymous with living. I need problems so badly that if problems didn't exist, I'd have to invent them. And I do.

Rudy would have put it better, as The Harder Law:

Once you eliminate your number one problem, YOU promote number two.

The ability to find the problem in any situation is the consultant's best asset. It's also the consultant's occupational disease. To be a consultant, you must detest problems, but if you can't live with problems, consulting will kill you.

Does this mean you must give up *trying* to solve problems? Not at all. It means that you must give up the illusion that you'll ever *finish* solving problems. Once you give up that illusion, you'll be able to relax now and then and let the problems take care of themselves.

People who can solve problems do lead better lives. But people who can ignore problems, when they choose to, live the best lives. If you can't do both, stay out of consulting.

The Hardest Law

Obviously, I'm sufficiently thick-skinned to accept failure and ignore problems. Otherwise, I'd be out of the consulting business by now, and I certainly wouldn't be writing a book about how to help others.

So, now I'll let you in on a big secret, the biggest one so far. I'm not writing this book for you, I'm writing it for *me*. In fact, that's also why I do all my consulting work, because trying to help others always winds up initially helping me more than it helps my clients.

A little poem I keep over my desk expresses this philosophy:

To make a bundle, be a star;
Spread it wide and spread it far.
But if you want to change the sun,
Best begin with Number One.

This may sound selfish and paradoxical, but in the end, it's neither. I can never be of maximum help to clients if my problems are tangled uncontrollably with theirs. So I try to get my own mess straightened out before tackling theirs.

Unfortunately, as my own behavior demonstrates:

Helping myself is even harder than helping others.

That's The Hardest Law, and that's essentially what this book is about.

2

cultivating
a paradoxical
frame of mind

We can do it—and this is how much it will cost.

The Urango Juice Toot

By now, you may have noticed that many of the laws of consulting take the form of paradoxes, dilemmas, and contradictions, and that they are often humorous. Perhaps this format has surprised you. Perhaps you thought that the consultant, of all people, must be logical, single-minded, and, above all, serious. Nothing could be further from the truth.

First of all, consultants deal in change. Most people—that is, most groups of people—function quite logically most of the time. And most of the time they don't need consultants. The time they do need a consultant is *when logic isn't working.* Usually they have arrived at some paradox, dilemma, or contradiction. They are, in a word, *stuck.*

WHY PARADOX?

"Stuck" reminds me of one of my "technical" consulting assignments when a computer was literally stuck. For no logical reason, the company's payroll program would start to process the record for the first employee and then would sit there, doing nothing—and doing it 10,000,000 times per second. The programmers confronted me with a long, logical list of reasons why this couldn't possibly be happening— but, of course, it *was* happening. And if the payroll wasn't computed in a few hours, there would be hell to pay.

Applying Sherby's Second Law of Consulting, I reasoned that there was a people problem. The most obvious people problem was that the programmers were in a panic that was petrifying their ability to think. All the logical things they had tried weren't working, so I decided to try something illogical. I fabricated a fictitious employee, Aaron Aardvark, who had done no work and who would be paid nothing. I put Aaron's time card up in front of the other time cards and reran the program. His time card was rejected—and rightly so—but the rest of the payroll ran perfectly.

If logic always worked, nobody would need consultants. So consultants always confront contradictions. That's why I advise consultants

Don't be rational; be reasonable.

Some consultants can't accept this advice. They want to know, for example, what the *logic* was behind Aaron Aardvark. I couldn't explain

21

the "logic" in advance of experimenting with the fictitious record, but I could explain why it was a *reasonable* thing to do. It was reasonable because the programmers were so paralyzed by logic that they couldn't think effectively. Thus, anything I did was quite likely to be an improvement. Aaron Aardvark was the first, simplest idea that popped into my head. If that hadn't worked, I would have tried something else.

Computer consultants may now find it unsettling that I don't intend to give any additional explanation of Aaron Aardvark, but I want them to experience their own reactions to paradox. Like all my readers, they will be exposed to many paradoxes in the following essays, not all of which can or should be explained.

Because I can't explain everything to them logically, some readers will resist the paradoxical and insist even more vehemently on being logical. Perhaps they would rather be right than effective.

Rational consultants are always tripped up when their clients start being illogical, because

People who think they know everything are easiest to fool.

When they do trip, these consultants try to cover themselves with high-sounding rationalizations. They seem to believe that their lack of humor will be interpreted as rationality. Typically, they fool only themselves.

In a paradoxical world, sooner or later everybody stumbles. It helps to understand why you stumble, but most important things can be explained only in jokes, riddles, and paradoxes. Survival requires that we learn to laugh things off and start over, which leads us to the next paradox:

The business of life is too important to be taken seriously.

OPTIMITIS AND THE TRADEOFF TREATMENT

> The Hatter opened his eyes very wide on hearing this; but all he *said* was, "Why is a raven like a writing-desk?"
>
> "Come, we shall have some fun now!" thought Alice. "I'm glad they've begun asking riddles—I believe I can guess that," she added aloud.

Alice probably suffered from the disease that affects so many consultants: the inability to resist solving problems. Not knowing Rudy's

Rutabaga Rule, Alice takes the Hatter's bait, and a mad conversation ensues. Eventually, Alice tries to stop:

> "Have you guessed the riddle yet?" the Hatter said, turning to Alice again.
>
> "No, I give it up," Alice replied. "What's the answer?"
>
> "I haven't the slightest idea," said the Hatter.
>
> "Nor I," said the March Hare.
>
> Alice sighed wearily. "I think you might do something better with the time," she said, "than wasting it in asking riddles that have no answers."
>
> "If you knew Time as well as I do," said the Hatter, "you wouldn't talk about wasting it. It's him."
>
> "I don't know what you mean," said Alice.

And then she was hooked again.

Alice wasn't the only one hooked by the riddle, which, according to Martin Gardner, became the object of much parlor speculation in Lewis Carroll's time. Eventually, Carroll wrote that the riddle, as originally invented, had no answer at all. But this didn't stop the speculation, which shouldn't surprise anyone who understands Rudy's Rutabaga Rule.

Every occupation has its characteristic diseases. Hatters in the 19th century were subject to mercury poisoning, which affected their brains; hence, the expression "mad as a hatter." The inability to resist solving problems is only one of the occupational diseases from which consultants suffer. Like hatters, they are subject to fits of madness, not from mercury, but sometimes from an excess of hot air. Many consultants pickle their livers at business lunches, blind their eyes on voluminous reports, or bend their spines in endless meetings. But the most serious occupational disease is known as *optimitis*.

Optimitis can be found in anyone who is asked to produce solutions to problems. It is an inflammation of the optimization nerve, that part of the nervous system which responds to such requests as

> "Give us the minimum cost solution."
> "Get it done in the shortest possible time."
> "We must do it in the best possible way."

In a healthy individual, the optimization nerve receives such requests and sends an impulse to the mouth to respond,

"What are you willing to sacrifice?"

In the diseased individual, however, this neural pathway is interrupted, and the mouth utters some distorted phrases like,

"Yes, boss. Right away, boss."

Tradeoff Charts

The social cost of optimitis runs large. Anyone who has ever been stuck implementing a project conceived by a diseased consultant will want to know the cure: a kind of physical therapy using what I call tradeoff charts.

Figure 2.1 is an example of a tradeoff chart that might be used to cure a consultant who has been given the problem: "Design the world's fastest runner." The chart is a graph of speed versus distance for world records in running events. All tradeoff charts are graphs of this type: one performance measure versus another. What they show is how one performance measure has to be traded off, in the real world, against some other.

In this case, speed has been traded against distance. Assuming that the world's record is about the best you can do at any given time, the curve of speed versus distance gives you something to shoot for in designing your solution. It also gives you an idea of the relationship between these two measures of performance, a relationship that may hold even for some newly designed runner.

The tradeoff chart indicates that if you want to run faster, you'll have to restrict yourself to a shorter distance, assuming that all other factors are kept the same. Alternatively, it says that you can run further if you're willing to go more slowly. But most important, it says,

You don't get nothin' for nothin'.

We call this message The Tradeoff Treatment.

If someone asks you to run faster, you can offer to do so, provided that you need not keep it up for such a long distance. Or, if a longer-distance runner is needed, you may be able to run farther, provided you're willing to go more slowly. But you're unlikely to get a faster runner who can run farther as well, nor will you find a longer-distance runner who runs faster.

Optimitis can be a confusing disease because people fail to recognize the limiting nature of the tradeoff chart. Figure 2.2 shows a plot of speed versus distance for a particular runner who is not a world record

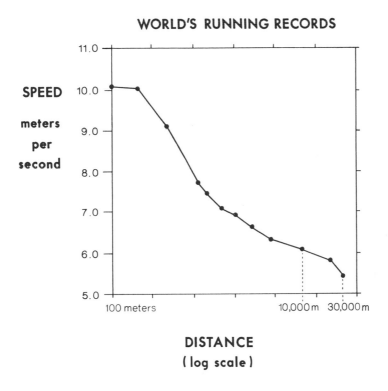

Figure 2.1. World's Running Records.

holder at any distance. Because the tradeoff chart is composed of world records, we know that runner X's plot will *never* surpass it. Runner X's curve represents a particular design relative to the best possible design on these two dimensions. Reading the curve, we can characterize runner X as a slow starter and not much of a sprinter, but with good endurance at long distances.

In Figure 2.3, we see another curve, this time for runner Y who might be characterized as a sprinter who cannot go the distance. In Figure 2.4, we see my own curve, which describes a lousy runner at all distances.

The Tradeoff Treatment

Seeing Figures 2.1 through 2.4, we begin to understand how The Tradeoff Treatment cures optimitis. When someone asks a diseased consultant to "design the fastest runner," conditioning through long therapy must trigger the reaction,

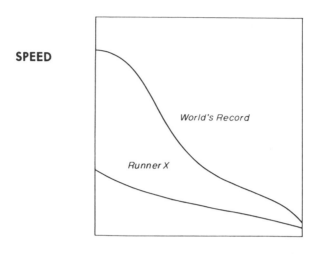

SPEED

World's Record

Runner X

DISTANCE

**Figure 2.2. Performance of a Long-Distance Runner
Compared with World Record Performances.**

"Let me check my tradeoff chart."

After creating the chart, the consultant will naturally think of responses such as the following:

1. What distance do you wish to work with?

2. It will be relatively easy to get a system that runs fast at 100 meters, if it doesn't ever have to run 30,000 meters very well.

3. We can easily find an off-the-shelf system, like GMW in Figure 2.4, which will lower the cost, but if you want world record performance, there aren't going to be many candidates at any distance.

4. If you need long distances, your 100 meter times may not be so good.

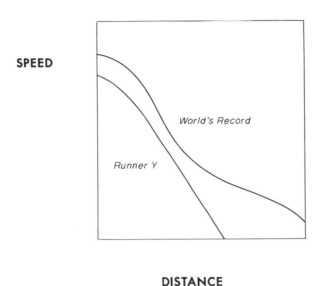

SPEED

**Figure 2.3. Performance of a Sprinter
Compared with World Record Performances.**

Once the questions start, there's a chance that the solution effort will be on a reasonable path, acknowledging that you don't get anything without paying for it.

The converse, unfortunately, is not true at all. You may very well pay for something and not get it. You may hire GMW at professional athlete rates, but even a million dollars won't get him running 100 meters in under 15 seconds. The healthy consultant spends time trying to get a healthy curve, not an impossible one.

There are many tradeoffs in any business, and the consultant must learn them and call them to the client's attention. There are also many *general* tradeoffs in the world, which form some of the great secrets of consulting. We'll discuss some of them presently, but before you get hung up in details, you should notice that all tradeoffs, to a first approximation, can be reduced to a tradeoff chart that's shaped like Figure 2.1. The labels may be different, the scales may be different, but the thinking is the same:

Moving in one direction incurs a cost in the other.

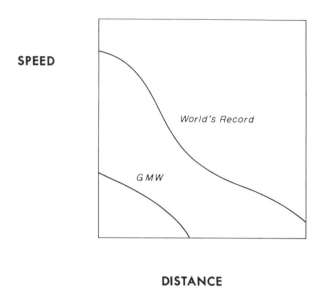

SPEED

DISTANCE

**Figure 2.4. Comparison of Gerald M. Weinberg's Performance
with World Record Performances.**

Until you learn to master the art of thinking in tradeoff terms, and then learn to juggle simultaneous tradeoffs, you'll never be a healthy consultant.

TIME TRADEOFFS

Once you've taken The Tradeoff Treatment, the world is never quite the same. Everywhere you look, you see tradeoffs. The other day I was relaxing in the garden, watching the bees kissing the flowers, when suddenly it occurred to me that flowers must strike just the right tradeoff if they want to keep the bees pollinating them. If a flower gives too little nectar, the bees will go to other flowers. But if the flower gives too much nectar, then the bee will get all it needs in a single visit, and not go spread pollen to other flowers. The amount of nectar must be a compromise between these two competing forces.

I went to the library to get a book about bees and flowers, but I had some difficulty with the librarian, who didn't want the book going out of the library. He seemed more concerned with preventing damage to or loss of the book than with getting me the information I needed. I was angry with him until I realized that librarians have their tradeoffs, too. In this case, it was a matter of present access (for me) versus future access (for others).

I decided to copy the pages I needed, which confronted me with another tradeoff: the cost of copying too much versus the cost of not having the pages I needed if I copied too little.

Now Versus Later

All three of the preceding tradeoffs—pollination, circulation, duplication—take the form of "now versus later." The problem of which pages to copy can be thought of as trading time now, when copying, for time later, when using the information. As with all now/later tradeoffs, there is the problem of balancing certainty now versus uncertainty in the future. If I knew for sure what I would need later, there would be no tradeoff problem.

Last week, one of my clients got angry about something I said in a meeting, and I didn't understand what her objection was. I had to make a decision: Deal with her anger now, which would take time from the meeting, or deal with it later. If I waited until later, the problem might just fade away, or it might fester and cost me much more time. I was aware of the tradeoff, and I decided to handle the problem by sharing my awareness with her—and with the others in the meeting, since their time was also involved. I said to her, "I'm aware that something I said doesn't agree with you. I don't want to ignore that, but we all have business to attend to in this meeting. Can you and I discuss this over lunch, or do you think it will interfere with the business of the meeting if we don't resolve it first?"

In effect, I was presenting the time tradeoff as a problem for all in the meeting to solve, which ran the risk of using even more time now. I tend to do that because I've learned that people underestimate future time when it's something that might be unpleasant, like dealing with an angry person. "Maybe it will go away" is the attitude, and, of course, sometimes it does. But on the average, it seems to pay to invest a little more time now at least to find out how much time it will take later. By making the time tradeoff explicit and by indicating a willingness to contribute time now, I make it clear that it is a problem of *limited time*, not a problem of *limited respect* for the other person.

Fisher's Fundamental Theorem

Many years ago, Sir Ronald Fisher noted that every biological system had to face the problem of present versus future, and that the future was always less certain than the present. To survive, a species had to do well today, but not so well that it didn't allow for possible change tomorrow. His Fundamental Theorem of Natural Selection said that the more adapted an organism was to present conditions, the less adaptable it tended to be to unknown future conditions.

We can apply the theorem to individuals, small groups of people, large organizations, organizations of people and machines, and even complex systems of machinery, and can generalize it as follows:

The better adapted you are, the less adaptable you tend to be.

I call this more general form of the law Fisher's Fundamental Theorem.

In my consulting, I'm often called upon to help establish recruiting policies. Inevitably, a decision must be made between hiring older people, who are more experienced in a particular skill, and younger people, who may prove more adaptable to learning new skills that may be required in the future. Again, my bias tends to be toward investing in the future, even at considerable sacrifice of present performance. I've found that people tend to overestimate the time it takes to acquire a skill, perhaps because they are seeking the *optimum* performance rather than something reasonably close to the optimum.

When working on training policies, I find the same tradeoff. People want training that makes them better adapted to the present task, rather than training that makes them more adaptable to future tasks. Perhaps their experience has told them that training that claims to be future-oriented is merely a different sort of specialized training, rather than training in adaptability. If you can't relate your training to anything, it's tempting to claim that it's training for everything. Perhaps it is a problem of risk: We just don't know what the future will bring.

Risk Versus Certainty

Economists have a technique for measuring the tradeoff between present certainties and future risks. The technique involves first establishing a mental game, then asking the players how much they would pay to play the game. Here's an example of the game:

> I toss a coin. If it comes up heads, I give you $2.10. If it comes up tails, I give you nothing. Now, consider how much you would pay to play the game.

Although the odds are evidently fifty-fifty, many people will not even pay a dollar to play this game. You can argue that, on the average, they will win $1.05 per play if they play many times, but they reply that they are not going to play many times, but only once. They prefer the sure dollar they already have to the $2.10 they *might* have, and will not risk having nothing.

Different people will offer different amounts to play the game. Some will offer $1.05, or even more, just for the fun of playing. That's why racetracks stay in business. Some will pay much less, and some will not play at any price. In my workshops, I have offered to play this game for a penny, only to find some people refuse. They say, "You're always tricking us, so even though it looks like a good deal, we know there's a trick somewhere. We won't be made fools of again." And, of course, by refusing an almost free chance of winning $2.10, they make fools of themselves. But, then, maybe I *was* going to trick them.

The Third-Time Charm

I used to be upset when my clients were so conservative about implementing my great ideas, especially when they seemed to promise great future payoffs for small present risks. Then one client pointed out that *my* risk, as consultant, was quite different from his: If my ideas kept being ignored, I would certainly lose my consulting contract. If they were implemented, I might be a hero, but even if everything flopped, I would merely lose the contract I was going to lose anyway.

His risk was quite different: If he did nothing, he wouldn't be any worse off than he was now. If he did what I suggested, he might be better off, but if my ideas flopped, he would be much worse off. With a secure job, he was well adapted to the present situation. With a shaky consulting contract, I was prepared to be much more adaptable, with *his* organization.

So Fisher's Fundamental Theorem provides one reason why people need consultants. Consultants are less adapted to the present situation, and therefore are potentially more adaptable. Their perception of now/then tradeoffs is different from those close to the problem, which makes them a valuable source of ideas, as well as people not to be trusted.

By working with a client for an extended period of time, it's possible to establish trust by recommending only low-risk alternatives. This strategy is another now/then tradeoff: small results now for the possibility of bigger results later. But later, the consultant will be better adapted to the situation, and thus less likely to provide a truly big idea.

These consulting tradeoffs may explain something I've observed in myself and other consultants.

Consultants tend to be most effective on the third problem you give them.

We call this The Third-Time Charm. Unfortunately, most clients don't seem to know about it, because they either drop you after one problem or retain you indefinitely. The Third-Time Charm is one secret of consulting that we ought to leak to our clients.

THE ORANGE JUICE TEST

In the long run, The Tradeoff Treatment is worth the effort. In the short run, however, it risks losing good consulting jobs. I used to worry that I would lose business to overly optimistic competitors, but with LeRoy's help, I got over it.

LeRoy was president of a custom software firm that had engaged my services to facilitate some problem-solving. For a couple of days, there was no break in the action, so I had little chance to talk to LeRoy. Eventually, the only alternative was to catch him for breakfast, which violates a hard and fast rule. If there's one thing worse than a business lunch, it's a business breakfast.

LeRoy shared my feelings, so we finished off the business part of the breakfast even before the waitress got around to warming up the first cup of coffee. As the food came, we settled back to enjoy the small talk, and the possibility of exchanging some really interesting information.

LeRoy asked me about the consulting business, and I asked him about the software business. LeRoy said we had many problems in common, especially the problem of not being able to predict if and when we would be awarded contracts. That gave me an opening.

"I'd be curious to know how come you gave *me* this contract," I asked. "But don't tell me if it would violate some confidence."

"Not at all," LeRoy assured me, raising his juice glass in a mock toast. "You got the contract because you were the only one who passed The Orange Juice Test."

"The Orange Juice Test? But how? Perhaps I shouldn't admit this, but I don't even drink orange juice. It gives me gas."

"Oh, The Orange Juice Test has nothing really to do with orange juice. It's just named after one particular application of the test in which it's used to select a conference hotel. But you can use the test for selecting any service."

"Like consultants?"

"Or software houses. Which is how I learned about it. One of *my* clients told me about it, when I asked her the same question."

"So how does it work?"

"Well, imagine that you had to choose a site for an annual sales convention, accommodating seven hundred people."

"I have some experience with that problem. It's not easy."

"Yes, but with The Orange Juice Test, you can do pretty well. At the very least, you can eliminate some of the losers."

"I'm all ears. How do you do it?"

LeRoy smiled over his coffee cup. "When you see the banquet manager for a hotel, you pose the following problem: The founder of your company has established a hallowed tradition for your sales meetings, requiring that each morning's sales breakfast start with a toast to success, using orange juice."

"A sales breakfast for seven hundred people?" I grimaced. "That's downright disgusting!"

"Oh, you don't really intend to have the breakfast. It's just part of the test. You then explain that the breakfast must start with the ceremony precisely at 7 a.m. . . . ."

" . . . that's even more revolting."

" . . . and that each of the seven hundred people must have a large glass of freshly squeezed orange juice."

"A *large* glass?"

"Yes, large. Not like this one, which they simply *call* large on the menu. But a drinking-glass size, at least."

"And *freshly squeezed?*"

"No more than two hours before serving."

"I see the problem."

"Well, that's the test. After posing this problem, you listen to what the banquet managers tell you."

"They'll probably say that it can't be done."

"That might happen," LeRoy said, "in which case they flunk The Orange Juice Test."

"But I know managers who would say, 'No problem,' just to get the business."

" . . . which also flunks The Orange Juice Test. They might be lying, or they might really think there's no problem. I don't know which is worse, but I don't want to have my convention at either place."

"So who passes?"

"The one who says what you said to us, when you took this job."

I was puzzled. "I don't remember discussing orange juice. What did I say?"

LeRoy smiled. "You said, 'That's a real problem. I can help you with it, . . . *and this is how much it will cost.'* So you passed The Orange Juice Test."

"But surely you considered more than that? No doubt I could get workers to squeeze oranges at 5 a.m. if I paid them a thousand dollars apiece. But would you be willing to pay that much?"

"I might, or I might not, but it's not for the banquet managers to decide that for me. That's my job, not theirs. If your price had been too high, we would have eliminated you, too. But that's a different test. There's no sense in getting a low price if they can't do the job, or if they're going to con you and give you canned orange juice in small glasses."

We finished breakfast and got back to work. I don't remember too much about how the consulting assignment turned out, but I'll never forget The Orange Juice Test, which I've restated as

We can do it—and this is how much it will cost.

I use the test every day. Whenever I want a service performed, I tell them what I want, they tell me how much it will cost to get it from them, and I decide whether it's worth it to me.

The Orange Juice Test has saved me hundreds of hours of haggling with the wrong people. I use it in service stations, in the office, in restaurants, and even in choosing hotels. I use it with my clients to treat our mutual optimitis about some plan that promises something for nothing. I also use it when *I* hire consultants.

3

being effective
when you don't know
what you're doing

LEVINE THE
GENIUS TAILOR

If you can't fix it, feature it.

—The Bolden Rule

Most consultants start out life as specialists. It's easier that way, but it does present a problem to their clients, as illustrated by the following fable.

THE PROBLEM WITH SPECIALISTS

The Elephant in the Boardroom

Sometime after the March meeting of the board of directors of Sylvan Forest Products, an elephant came out of the forest and moved into the boardroom. Nobody noticed, until the September meeting when the managing director couldn't open the door. "There's something in there," said the managing director, "and it's blocking the door."

Peering under the door, the comptroller saw the shadow of the elephant's feet. "It looks as if some trees have grown inside. Better send for the silviculturist."

The silviculturist managed to splinter the fine oak door partway open with his peavey, but the elephant leaned to one side and slammed it shut again. "I don't think it's trees," said the silviculturist. "It's a huge gray monster—more like a whale."

The board then sent for a cetaceanologist, who advised them to flood the boardroom so that the whale could swim out. But as the room filled with water, the elephant simply blew it out with her trunk through the broken door. Seeing the trunk, the cetaceanologist said, "No wonder it doesn't swim out. It's not a whale at all, but a large snake."

Next, the board summoned an ophiologist, who advised, "Toss in some burning oily rags. That will drive out any snake." But the elephant simply stamped out the flames as fast as the burning rags could be thrown through the door. The board decided to call the janitor to clear the anteroom of splintered wood, muddy water, and oily, smoked furniture.

The janitor asked about the mess. After the managing director told the story, he reached in his pocket and pulled out some peanuts. When he held one through the door, the elephant—which was by this time mightily hungry—grabbed it with her trunk. "Come on, Little One," the janitor coaxed, holding out the other peanuts, and in a moment, the elephant lumbered out the door. After feasting a while on peanuts, she shyly retreated to the forest.

"But how did you know it was an elephant?" the astonished comptroller asked.

"Oh, I didn't know. I only suspected because it was partly like a forest, partly like a whale, and partly like a snake. It was only a theory, so I figured it would be better to risk one of my peanuts than to cause further damage to your boardroom."

Out of Your Depth

If you had an elephant in your boardroom, which specialist would you call? The toughest problems don't come in neatly labeled packages. Or they come in packages with the wrong labels. That's why they're so tough.

Three times out of four, consultants find themselves asked to work on problems that aren't really their "specialty." The consultant just looks like a specialist to a nonspecialist. But good consultants can handle many of those problems anyway, because in addition to being specialists, they are problem-solvers. If you dig into their bag of tricks, you'll find that their best ones have nothing whatsoever to do with their specialties, but can be used by consultants in any field.

We'll start our survey of such tricks with a set of tricks that not only can be applied when you're working out of your field, but when you're working out of your depth.

MARVIN'S MEDICAL SECRETS

Every profession has its secrets. Although *ours* must be kept secret, any secret from a different profession appeals to our prurient interests. And of all the secrets, medical secrets are undoubtedly the juiciest. Unlike most people, I'm blessed with a brother-in-law, Marvin, who's a doctor, and a rather cynical one at that. He's willing to tell me, an outsider, some of the great secrets of medicine.

In medicine, Marvin assures me that The First Great Secret is

Ninety percent of all illness cures itself—with absolutely no intervention from the doctor.

Because of this great secret, all the doctor must do is follow Hippocrates and avoid harming the patient. Well, almost all. A successful doctor must also convince the patient that something is being done to cure the disease, something that could only come from the vast store of esoteric medical knowledge. Otherwise, there would soon be doctors on the breadlines.

The reason that ninety percent of all illness cures itself lies in "the wisdom of the body." Although "wisdom" sounds mysterious, it's merely a poetical summary of the end result of thousands of generations of destructive testing, carried on in thousands of millions of individuals. Most of those tests were without benefit of modern medicine, so any body design that didn't have the wisdom to cure itself was summarily removed from the population. Each of us, after all, is the direct descendant of innumerable unbroken lines of survivors.

The First Great Secret

Can this medical secret be translated to apply in other consulting practices? It all depends on the system the consultant is trying to "cure." If the system has a long history of practice in curing itself, then the consultant should lean toward the "do no harm" approach. For instance, people have been working in small groups for thousands of years, so they can be expected to have certain inbred skills at curing group ills. They may occasionally get into trouble that prompts them to call a consultant, but the trouble is likely to be "cured" by the gentlest possible intervention, perhaps by patient waiting.

In contrast, we don't expect that computers will have any "wisdom" at all. If a consultant is called to cure one, the remedy might have to be quite direct and harsh, like amputating memory. Since Sherby says "it's always a people problem," the consultant should consider the people who are ordinarily responsible for keeping the computer well. If the computer *plus* those people are considered the "body," then you can expect a certain amount of wisdom, and temper your prescription accordingly.

In short, we can adapt Marvin's First Great Secret to say

Deal gently with systems that should be able to cure themselves.

Clearly, Marvin's laws are quite general, and not restricted to medicine. His First Great Secret, for instance, is well-known to engineers as The First Law of Engineering:

If it ain't broke, don't fix it.

Any system that ain't sick should be able to cure itself.

The Second Great Secret

According to Marvin, the second secret of medicine has to do with penicillin. Of the ten percent of illnesses that don't cure themselves, penicillin or some other antibiotic handily dispatches another ninety percent. Contrary to popular belief, however, antibiotics alone aren't sufficient. They must be used properly, and that's where the doctor earns that fat fee.

For instance, indiscriminate popping of penicillin pills every time you have a cold violates Marvin's First Great Secret. The common cold is one of the ninety percent of illnesses the body is wise enough to cure by itself, so the penicillin does no good whatsoever. It might be of psychological assistance, but any inert pill would provide that. Moreover, penicillin most decidedly is not inert. Even though it's not affecting the cold, it is affecting other things. In some people, penicillin provokes an allergic reaction, sometimes leading to death; at the very least, each use of it affects the body's sensitivity to penicillin, so that someday when it's *really* needed, it may have little or no effect, which leads us to Marvin's Second Great Secret:

Repeatedly curing a system that can cure itself will eventually create a system that can't.

This secret should be branded on the bottom of every parent who ever wiped the nose of a child over the age of four, and on the forehead of any consultant who makes a living solving the same problem for the same client, over and over.

The Third Great Secret

Any drug as strong as penicillin is bound to create problems. Some people are so worried about taking unnecessary drugs that they stop taking their antibiotics too soon. Rather than complete the prescribed course of treatment, they stop if the most obvious and uncomfortable symptoms don't disappear immediately. In the case of bacterial infections, these symptoms may remain even though the offending organisms are being brought under control. But if the treatment stops too soon, the disease springs back, and this time it's probably resistant to the antibiotic.

Marvin's Third Great Secret says

Every prescription has two parts: the medicine and the method of ensuring correct use.

Marvin says he learned this secret traveling in France, where he ate an entire box of suppositories. I learned it from a dozen clients, where I neglected to contract for consulting to follow-up on my suggestions.

The Fourth Great Secret

Marvin is not merely a plain old M.D.; he is a psychiatrist. Of all the medical gossip, no gossip is more fascinating to me than the stories about crazy people. The story that follows, however, is not about crazy people but about psychiatrists, who everyone knows can't possibly be crazy.

Once a month, Marvin drives to the state mental hospital to consult with staff physicians on their most intransigent cases. Marvin says that this kind of consulting is his easiest work, because he really doesn't have to know any medicine or psychiatry at all. Whenever they bring out one of their tough cases, Marvin merely asks them what treatment they've been using. If they say treatment A, he tells them to switch to treatment B. If they tell him treatment B, he switches treatment to A. Oh, he surrounds all this with suitable mumbo jumbo (doctors are the easiest marks for their own medicine), but the principle is simple and powerful enough to be Marvin's Fourth Great Secret:

If what they've been doing hasn't solved the problem, tell them to do something else.

Actually, The Fourth Great Secret was long known to Dr. Krankheit, the great vaudeville comedian, whose skit would go like so: A patient would come in and say, "Dr. Krankheit, it hurts when I turn my head like this."

Krankheit would gaze at the poor sufferer and say, with infinite medical wisdom in his voice, "Don't turn your head like that!"

The Fifth Great Secret

Dr. Krankheit's Cure, as The Fourth Great Secret is also known, provides a technique that should work for any consultant. Because Marvin's a consultant, the only cases he sees are the problems the hospital doctors aren't solving by themselves. Therefore, one thing Marvin knows for sure is that *whatever* they're doing, it isn't right. They've become stuck on one approach and can't get unstuck. He also knows that this system only works if they're paying him a large fee, which leads to The Fifth Great Secret:

Make sure they pay you enough so they'll do what you say.

Another way to state this is

The most important act in consulting is setting the right fee.

This is such an important secret that I devote all of Chapter 12 to it.

The Sixth Great Secret

There's no question that *any* consultant can use The Fifth Great Secret. There's so much we can learn from one another by sharing secrets, but we can learn even more by examining a few of the secrets side by side. For instance, two of the secrets say, in effect

Don't give up the treatment too soon. Don't stick with the treatment too long.

So, perhaps there's another good reason for those huge fees. The secret of their secrets lies not in the secrets themselves, but in knowing when to apply each one, which is The Sixth Great Secret:

Know-how pays much less than know-when.

Vaudeville comedians like Dr. Krankheit can take the most stupid joke and make you bust your gut laughing. In jokes, as in consulting, timing is everything. A good joke is crazy behavior done at the right time. And Marvin says that "crazy" behavior is nothing more nor less than "normal" behavior done beyond its useful range. For a consultant, "clever" behavior is "crazy" behavior done when it works.

FEATURING FAILURE

Once upon a time, a man went to Levine the Tailor because he heard that he could get a cheap, custom-made suit. When the suit was finished and he went to try it on, it didn't fit him at all. "Look," he said, "the jacket is much too big in back."

"No problem," replied Levine, showing him how to hunch his back to take up the slack in the jacket.

"But then what about the right arm? It's three inches too long."

"No problem," Levine repeated, demonstrating how, by leaning to one side and stretching out his right arm, the sleeve could be made to fit.

"And what about these pants? The left leg is too short."

"No problem," said Levine for the third time, and he proceeded to teach him how to pull up his leg at the hip so that, although he limped badly, the suit appeared to fit.

Having no more complaints, the man set off hobbling down the street, feeling slightly duped by Levine. Before he went two blocks, he was stopped by a stranger, who said, "I beg your pardon, but is that a new suit you're wearing?"

The man was pleased that someone had noticed his suit, so he took no offense. "Yes, it is," he replied. "Why do you ask?"

"Well, I'm in the market for a new suit myself. Who's your tailor?"

"It's Levine—right down the street."

"Well, thanks very much," said the stranger, hurrying off. "I do believe I'll go to Levine for *my* suit. Why, he must be a genius to fit a cripple like you!"

The Bolden Rule

Whenever I'm telling stories to a group of computer programmers, someone insists on hearing about Levine. I feel like Lewis Carroll spinning *Alice's Adventures in Wonderland* to Alice Liddell, who delighted in recognizing herself as the story's protagonist.

In Wonderland, whenever Alice found something topsy-turvy, she tended to blame herself, as any proper young lady has been taught to do. But in the wonderland of computers, where so *much* goes topsy-turvy, programmers need a less threatening strategy. That's why they adore Levine.

Levine couldn't sew a straight seam, but rather than try to fix it, or learn to do better, he adopted The Bolden Rule:

If you can't fix it, feature it.

After producing a few cripples, he didn't hang his head. Instead, he hung a sign: "Levine the Genius Tailor—Specializing in Cripples."

Although programmers pride themselves on their ability to feature their failures, they have no exclusive hold on The Bolden Rule. Here are some random examples taken from all walks of life:

- There are certain parts of a slaughtered animal that meat packers have never been able to induce people to eat, so they put them in sausages and hot dogs. Rather than hide this fact, one company advertises, "Our hot dogs are made with special cuts of meat."

- Motel designers have never quite figured out how to design bathrooms. Bathrooms with windows would require using precious space in outside walls, so they tried installing exhaust fans. But exhaust-fan designers don't seem able to make a cheap fan that's effective at

taking the moisture out of a tiny room with a shower.
So, motels feature "luxury heat lamps in all bathrooms."

- In the early 19th century, well-drillers were looking for
water or salt. Unfortunately, in too many cases, their
wells were ruined when they struck petroleum instead. Eventually, G.H. Bissell decided to see what use
could be made of this gummy stuff. By distilling it, he
was able to produce such useful products as illuminat-
ing gas, paraffin wax, lubricants, and lamp oil, so he
renamed these failures oil wells and proceeded to
make a fortune.

    Even so, the oil business wasn't all roses. In addition
    to these useful products, the distillation process pro-
    duced a useless and dangerous product called "gaso-
    line." It took a few more years before someone de-
    cided to apply The Bolden Rule one more time.

- Medicine has always known The Bolden Rule. Rather
frequently, a medicine is developed that turns out to
have some unacceptable side effect. Rather than throw
away all that research, the side effect is proclaimed as
the main effect, and the drug becomes a "wonder
drug." For example, a high blood pressure medicine caused copious growth of hair as a side effect,
so it was relabeled as a wonderful new cure for
baldness.

    In a different case, a patient is diagnosed as having
    "incurable cancer," and is given no more than a year
    to live. Nineteen years later, after moderate treatment,
    the alive and healthy patient is presented to the public
    as "a modern miracle of medical therapy," rather than
    as "a failure of diagnosis."

- Then there are bananas. People refused to buy fruit with
ugly dark spots, so a massive campaign placed Chiquita
Banana on every radio. Chiquita sang a song about
bananas—that "when they are *flecked with brown* and
have that golden hue, bananas taste the best and are the
best for you."

    The public swallowed Chiquita's banana message with
    gusto, but even more impressive is the slogan sold by
    poorly managed restaurants to their stuffy patrons.

"Good food takes time," they say, and who can doubt
it? But it also takes time to scorch the sauce.

The list could go on forever: The theater at which a bomb is playing
advertises "plenty of good seats available." The drug company whose
product is not as potent as the competition's advertises "more medicine
in each capsule." The politician unable to understand legislation becomes "one of the common people, guarding our freedoms from those
Harvard professors." The inept manufacturer proudly emphasizes that
extra long delivery times "give the customer time to prepare for the new
machine," while the company that can't sell its inventory stresses
"immediate delivery."

The Bolden Rule in Consulting

There's no question that The Bolden Rule is self-serving, but that
doesn't necessarily mean that it's harmful. Consultants who are repelled
by this self-serving aspect may miss many opportunities to use The
Bolden Rule to help their clients. Let me give a few examples from my
own work.

One client asked me to help him improve his shop's turnaround
time, explaining that program test runs were not being returned to the
programmers fast enough. Long turnaround time sometimes meant
that frustrated programmers would release programs before removing
all their errors, which was quite costly. After studying the system for
shortcuts, however, I was stumped. Unless the client was willing to
spend more than a million dollars on new equipment, I couldn't
shorten the turnaround time by more than an insignificant few
minutes.

Instead of branding myself a failure, I convinced them that their
real problem was not turnaround time, but errors. I changed the name
from turnaround time to "think time," and taught the programmers
techniques for using this special period for reducing the number of
errors. With fewer errors to find, they needed fewer test runs, so
turnaround time didn't affect them that much. Before I had even finished training them, some programmers had actually started to complain that they got their jobs back too quickly.

Calling turnaround time "think time" was certainly self-serving. It
concealed the fact that I wasn't smart enough to solve their technical
problems, but it also gave them more than their money's worth. The
purpose of consulting is not to make me look smart, but it's not to make
me look dumb either. Consulting is not a test for the consultant, it's a
service to the client.

Featuring Your Own Failures

Sometimes, though, it's hard to remember that you're not being tested, especially with certain clients. When I'm goaded often enough with the same question or remark, I sometimes lose my temper. In one meeting with a client group, an engineer named Arnie kept saying "I already tried that, and it didn't work" to every suggestion made by me or anyone else in the room. Finally, I blew up. "You seem to have tried everything else, Arnie. Why don't you try shutting up when someone makes a suggestion."

There was a dead silence in the room, and I could see that I had made a dreadful mistake. In one moment of weakness, I had destroyed my carefully constructed image as a calm facilitator of the meeting. Rather than give up a good client without a fight, I calmed myself and said, "Well, now you see that I'm not perfect. I lost my temper, and I'm sorry. It really hurts my feelings to have all my ideas turned down without a hearing, and I suspect that other people feel that way, too."

I saw several nods of agreement, so I continued. "Arnie, you have a habit of saying that every idea has been tried and didn't work. I don't doubt that you're correct, but perhaps the ideas of this committee don't have to be perfect, any more than I have to be perfect. I try to keep my temper, but every once in a while it doesn't work. Does that mean I shouldn't try again?"

Arnie looked puzzled. "Of course not. I didn't mean you shouldn't try those ideas. I just meant to give you the information that I knew some conditions under which they wouldn't work. I was trying to encourage everyone to keep refining their ideas."

So we taught Arnie to say, instead, "That's a great idea, and it ought to work really well once we take care of these few conditions." After the meeting, one of the other members took me aside and complimented me on my brilliant intervention. "If I didn't know better," she said, "I'd have sworn you really lost your temper at Arnie. You're one cool consultant."

In such cases, it's better to be open about having really failed, but nothing I said could change her mind. That's one risk of applying The Bolden Rule: People may begin to believe you're perfect (which isn't too bad, as long as you don't start believing it yourself).

FAKING SUCCESS

When you fly as much as I do, you sometimes want a bit of privacy. In order to prevent unwanted conversation from fellow passengers, my friend Daniel tells his seatmate that he slaughters pigs, but I think my cover story is better: "I sell used cars." People might talk voluntarily to a pig-sticker—but to a car salesman? Hardly ever.

Masquerading as a traveling used car salesman has caused me to give more thought to this much maligned occupation: I don't believe car salesmen deserve undisputed last place in the human race, and I'd like to set the record straight.

I will concede that used car salesmen overuse The Bolden Rule. For example, if the car is extremely old, it's a "classic." If it guzzles gas, it's for "personal luxury." And it's never "used," but, rather, is "previously owned," or "experienced." Even so, you'll seldom catch a used car salesman telling an out-and-out lie—unless it's essential to making the sale. So before we banish salesmen to last place, we ought to take a look at the techniques used by some of the less imaginative professions. Like politicians.

Newspeak

Suppose the Banana Republic of Pygmia decides to pick on Gargantua, which is fifty times its size. Naturally, Gargantua sends in the marines. But Pygmia won't play by the rules of modern warfare, so the war drags on.

Unable to admit his mistake or remedy the situation, the President of Gargantua tells his nation that war is the best way to rebuild the moral fiber of the nation and to use up the stockpile of obsolete weapons. Besides, it's a good place to practice with new ones.

Soon the stockpiles are depleted, replaced with stockpiles of dead bodies. The nation is no longer willing to swallow these features, and the President has run out of imagination. So, he lies. On national television, he announces, "We won the War." All the marines, tanks, and guns are massed into a grand parade and marched in triumph out of Pygmia. The bottomless quagmire becomes the Great Victory of the Forces of Good over the Forces of Evil.

In the novel *1984*, George Orwell called this technique "newspeak," and depicted a society in which politicians relied on newspeak to the exclusion of other approaches. But real politicians aren't so dishonest; I believe they sincerely try to apply The Bolden Rule, but politicians seem to lack the car salesman's imagination. They use newspeak only because they can't make anything else work.

The Gilded Rule

Besides, why pick only on salesmen and politicians? The people who name real-estate developments are also devoted to The Gilded Rule:

If you can't feature it, fake it.

Their version is sometimes called The Pinebrook Ploy. Suppose a development lacks some desirable feature, such as trees or water. Rather than spend the money to put in a pond or stream, and rather than wait forty years while trees grow around the newly built houses, the developer simply creates a name suggesting the missing features.

Out here in the Nebraska prairie, where trees are scarcer than water, water is scarcer than hills, and the lay of the land lets you see for miles in every direction, there's no shortage of words describing desirable features. Everywhere you drive, you see signs directing you to Pinebrooks, Chestnut Highlands, Cottonwood Pond, Maple Glade, Willow Knolls, Aspen Meadows, Beechwood Shores, Elm Creek Hills, Oakmont Cascade. . . .

But why go on? The Pinebrook Ploy is so universally practiced that you can give odds that Oakmont Cascade contains neither oak, nor mountain, nor cascade, unless you count the stream that flows through your cellar. Besides, developers are no more guilty than technologists. Early proponents of gas lighting declared that gas light had the same healthful properties as sunlight. Under this application of The Gilded Rule, anyone forcing children to work twelve hours a day in a gas-lit factory was actually a great humanitarian. Without factory work, those children might not get the benefits of light on cloudy days.

X-rays, in their early days, were highly touted for their healthful powers, especially for curing cancer. The advocates of X-rays actually knew nothing about curing cancer, but they did know how to build X-ray machines.

So, what's the harm in a little gilding? I would observe that as with X-rays, which can be used either to cause or cure cancer, most new technologies can go either way—cause or cure. According to their advocates, computers were going to end boring, repetitious office work. Then how did computers become *synonymous* with boring, repetitious, trivial work? Certainly not because it's impossible to use a computer to make work more interesting, more stimulating, more significant.

Then why? Because faking always seems so much easier than fixing. Computers were gilded so enthusiastically, nobody bothered to find out what factors *make* a computer system boring or interesting, repetitious or stimulating, trivial or significant. And that's the danger when we smooth-talking consultants use The Gilded Rule. Once fakery works, we stop learning how to do real fixery.

The Inverse Gilded Rule

Should consultants ever use The Gilded Rule? Should you do unto others before they do unto you? Whenever I'm tempted to do so, I think of Abraham Lincoln. Although a politician, Abe was famous for his honesty, which was characterized by his favorite riddle: "If you call a tail a leg, how many legs does a dog have?" After his guests had variously guessed one or five, Lincoln would proclaim, "No. The answer is four. Calling it a leg doesn't make it a leg."

I'm ashamed to confess that when I was younger, I gilded quite a few tales. The reason I now spend so much of my time trying to remove the gilt is to remove the guilt. For instance, computer programmers are in the habit of gilding their mistakes by calling them bugs. (I know because I perpetuated this newspeak in my early technical books.) As long as we call mistakes bugs, they sound as if they just crawled spontaneously into our programs, which means we take no more responsibility for them than for other acts of nature.

Nowadays, when a client asks for my assistance in improving program quality, I always make a point of correcting everyone who speaks of bugs. Pretty soon, they're all saying "errors" or "mistakes," and half the battle is won. It's gotten so I can actually identify many client problems by the gilded language used to describe the problems. Clients who use euphemisms are hiding something—even from themselves. For example, most of the time, cost-benefit analysis means cost analysis, and no attention is paid to benefits. In plain language, this means "we're going to list every expense we can possibly associate with this plan, to make sure it's smothered."

Another example: While working on a problem of employee turnover, I heard the personnel manager speak of "flexibility," a fine-sounding word that to him meant "freedom to fire people if I don't like them, or if I have to cut labor expenses." That sort of terminology used to make me angry. Now it just gives me information I can use to improve the situation. All that's necessary is to apply The Inverse Gilded Rule:

If something's faked, it must need fixing.

In the example above, the cavalier attitude of the personnel manager was matched by the employees, who reasoned, "If management can fire those other people so easily, I could be the next one to go. If I get a halfway decent offer, I'll beat them to it." It takes a lot of work to break this cycle, but the first step is always the same: Stop using fake terms like "flexibility" and start calling things by their right name.

The Gilded Consultant

Most people instinctively apply The Inverse Gilded Rule to their consultants. If they catch you lying, they'll figure out that you must have something to hide. Even if it merely *sounds* like you're lying, you're in trouble. We consultants ought to bend over backward to understate our qualifications, but insecurity makes us all victim to occasional exaggeration.

A few years ago, a very wise consultant heard me bragging about how many books I had written. She quietly took me aside and suggested that I would be a more effective consultant if I didn't work so hard at labeling myself as a famous author.

"But I am famous," I protested, still full of myself, "at least in some circles. Do they think I'm lying?"

"It doesn't matter one way or the other. If they think you're lying, then they'll discount you, and won't follow your suggestions. If they think you're telling the truth, they'll discount *themselves*, and won't follow your suggestions. Do you see that?"

I had to agree, so she continued. "Well, if you're not doing it to help them, who are you trying to help? And if you need help so badly, you should be the client, not the consultant."

I think that's when I started telling people I was a used car salesman.

4

seeing what's there

**The child who receives a hammer for Christmas
will discover that everything needs pounding.**
—The Law of the Hammer

$\mathbf{A}$re you offended by the idea of general tools for consultants in different specialties? By suggesting general tools, I don't mean to imply that you need nothing else, but rather that you're in danger if you have too narrow a repertoire.

For one thing, there's The Law of the Hammer, which says

The child who receives a hammer for Christmas will discover that everything needs pounding.

The specialist who has only one tool may wind up hammering screws. Often, though, it's not the consultant who brings out special tools, but the client who insists on them. In my work with computing firms, they always want me to solve problems by using computer programs. If I suggest an approach that doesn't require using a computer at all, they can't believe it's worth anything.

Inventing a Tool to Improve Vision

Use of special tools can also cramp your ability to invent new tools on the spot. Some years ago, I worked with a software firm that wanted to improve poor product quality. The manager couldn't really define poor quality, except that he was "getting a lot of complaints."

"How many complaints are 'a lot,'" I asked, and was given a pile of letters about two feet high. I glanced at a few, then suggested, "Let's tabulate these complaints to see which products get the most."

"Great idea!" he said. "I can see why you're in such demand. I'll get us a programmer."

"What for?"

"To write the tabulation program, of course."

"That won't be necessary," I said.

He looked puzzled, then suddenly brightened. "Oh, you already have your own program. Of course."

"Not exactly," I replied, "but you have the tools we need right here in your office." I motioned to his map of North America, with a little red pin marking each client. "Do you have any extra pins?

53

He looked puzzled again, but handed me a box of pins. I removed some items from his bulletin board, tacked up a blank sheet of paper, and asked him for the names of all of his software products. For each name, I drew a box on the paper. Then I asked him to read the first letter from the pile of complaints. As soon as the letter mentioned the product name, I stuck a pin in that box and told him to skip to the next letter. In about fifteen minutes, we had a clear picture of which products were causing most of the trouble.

The manager was impressed, but clearly would have been happier with a program. I suggested that now that I had the information I needed, he might want to have someone write a program to tabulate future complaints. That made him happy, and I went to work to study the quality problem by studying how the most troublesome product was produced.

The pin technique, which I "invented" on the spot, was so successful that I added it to my tool kit. It's a wonderfully simple tool, far more readily available than computer programs for visualizing information that's heaped up in an unorganized fashion. But there are actually simpler tools than pins and a pinboard that all consultants can use when they need to see what's there that other people aren't seeing.

THE STUDY OF HISTORY

A Long, Yeasty Story

The vernal sunlight played on the white linen as Sparks absorbed the details of the executive dining room, the first day of his promotion to head up marketing.

"Do you like what you see?" Wilfram asked.

"The decor is better than I imagined, but the breadbasket surprised me."

"The breadbasket?"

"A few crackers and some sliced, standard American white bread. I'd always imagined executives would eat something tastier than raw dough."

"Your first day as a management consultant, and you're surprised already."

"Oh, that's not the first surprise," Sparks said, buttering another slice. "I spent the morning studying the organization of the marketing department."

"Did you like what you found?"

"Like it? You must be kidding! First of all, the people are all wrong. Second, the department is organized so poorly that even good people wouldn't help. I could make a better department with my eyes closed."

Wilfram sighed. "Oh, I'm sorry to hear that. I've always been rather proud of the way my plan for that department has held up over all these years."

"*Your* plan?"

"Yes. Like you, when I got my first promotion, I was assigned to head up marketing."

Sparks feared for his short consulting career—four hours on his first job and he'd just offended his client. He decided to change the subject. "I don't know why they can't bake a better bread. This stuff is almost unfit for human consumption. Where do they get it? From the penitentiary?"

"Actually, it's Mrs. Oldenhauser's bread."

"Then maybe they ought to put Mrs. Oldenhauser in the penitentiary."

"Oh, I don't know. Myrna Oldenhauser is a fine lady. She and I are on the Board of the Widows and Orphans Fund."

Sparks snatched another slice and started buttering furiously.

Wilfram rescued him with a smile. "Would you like to hear the story of Mrs. Oldenhauser's white bread?" Sparks nodded, his mouth stuffed with bread, so Wilfram commenced. "Jack and Myrna Oldenhauser used to be neighbors of mine, many years ago when we were all poor. Myrna was a fanatic about nutrition, but she couldn't afford the kind of food she wanted, so she started to bake her own bread."

He paused and sighed wistfully. "It was *beautiful* bread. I can remember how the neighbors always managed to visit her kitchen just as the first batch was coming out of the oven. Mmmmmnh, I can still taste it!

"Because it was so delicious, some of us asked Myrna to bake extra loaves. We paid her, of course, and she sorely needed that little extra money. After a while, other neighbors tasted the bread at our houses, and soon Myrna had to turn down further requests because her oven was operating full-time.

"For Christmas that year, Jack bought Myrna a new double oven so she could expand her clientele. By this time, the children were spending all of their spare time baking, so Myrna hired Winona Jenkins to help her out.

"Then, the local grocery started having trouble keeping up with Myrna's demands for high-quality ingredients, so she got in touch with a wholesaler. She had to compromise a tiny bit on quality, but the commercial grades were all she could get regularly in sufficiently large quantity.

"A few months after she bought her first delivery truck, traffic was so great she had to move her business to a commercial zone. I didn't see Myrna much after that, but she called me once to help her redesign her management structure for personnel, purchasing, accounts receivable, and distribution.

"I do recall that she had some reservations about baking the bread a day in advance, and underbaking at that. But she had to do something to keep it fresh on the shelves between deliveries. She didn't *want* to add preservatives, but her delivery pipeline was so long, she had no alternative.

"In order to provide stability for her employees, she needed to incorporate and add sales volume. Now she owns the biggest bakery in the state, and her bread is on the table in thousands of restaurants and homes."

The White Bread Warning

A computer consultant, reading this long, yeasty tale, remarked, "It seems a bit too stretched out for the point. And what was the point, anyway?" Like young Sparks, he has a lot to learn about listening to clients tell stories. For one thing, he has to learn about patience. For another, he has to learn about The Fallacy of the Single Point.

When Sparks decided that Wilfred had finally finished, he was sure he understood the point of the story. "That's quite a success story!" he said. "I'm sorry I said those things about Mrs. Oldenhauser and her bread."

"Why? You were exactly right. The stuff tastes like undercooked starch pudding."

"But I thought Mrs. Oldenhauser was your friend."

"She *is* my friend, but that doesn't mean I have to eat her white bread. She doesn't even eat it herself. She has a live-in cook."

"Then, what *is* the point of the story?"

"Well, one point is that a new consultant might have an easier time if he thought once in a while about The White Bread Warning."

"The White Bread Warning? What's that?"

"If you use the same recipe, you get the same bread."

"Everybody knows *that*."

"I suppose everyone does. But people don't always *remember* the warning when they most need it. I still recall Myrna Oldenhauser on the first day she decided to bake her own bread. We were in her kitchen, tasting some of the bread sold by Mrs. Wellington's bakery, when I asked Myrna if she liked it.

"'Like it?' she said. 'You must be kidding! First of all, the ingredients are all wrong. Second, it's baked so poorly even good ingredients wouldn't help. I could bake better bread with my eyes closed.'"

"So *that's* the point. She should have studied the evolution of Mrs. Wellington's operation before plunging into her own."

"That's funny," Wilfram mused. "I recall suggesting that myself."

"Did she do it?"

"Myrna? No, as I recall, she said that Mrs. Wellington ought to be put in the penitentiary."

"Ouch! I think I finally got your message. But I was already planning to ask your opinion on how to organize the marketing department."

"Then you didn't get my message at all. If I *knew* how to organize that department properly, I would have done it myself. If you're going to repeat *my* mistakes, why should I retain you?"

"You mean I *shouldn't* ask you how you did it?"

"No, you should certainly ask me how I *did* it. Just don't ask me how to *do* it, because all I've learned is what *not* to do. . . . Oh, good. Here comes the crab cocktail!"

Boulding's Backward Basis

Somewhere in this happy land, there is a Mrs. Halliburton starting yet another white-bread cycle. If she only had a consultant to study the history of Mrs. Oldenhauser, she might achieve a different outcome. She might avoid mistakes. She might detect small but important changes that Mrs. Oldenhauser overlooked. She might keep what worked and change what came out poorly.

But the most important thing Mrs. Halliburton could learn from Mrs. Oldenhauser is that Mrs. Oldenhauser failed to study history, and thus repeated it. As Gertrude Stein once remarked, "History teaches history teaches." But unless you study it, history teaches nothing.

Most people, like Sparks, are too impatient to study history. That's why studying history is a good way for consultants to see things that others have missed. The consultant who studies history can learn to avoid mistakes, capture missed opportunities, keep what worked, and change what had no effect. The consultant can learn about the environment, too, for even though the system is to be changed, it will have to survive in the environment experienced by the former system.

In short, the consultant studies history because, as the economist Kenneth Boulding says,

Things are the way they are because they got that way.

This rule is so important to consultants that I've given it a special name, Boulding's Backward Basis. Any time you're on a new consulting assignment and need to become acquainted with the situation in a hurry, try using Boulding's Backward Basis. To do so, you may have to slow down and listen to a client's long, boring, irrelevant story.

Sparks's Law of Problem Solution

But even if the stories actually turn out to be irrelevant, there may be important political reasons for beginning with a historical survey: The people who were part of the process that produced the problem are still around and will be involved, in one way or another, in the attempts to solve it.

But don't commit the mistake made by young Sparks: It's not always a good idea to see everything, or, if you do see it, to comment on everything. If you loudly castigate the people who were responsible for producing the present mess, you may then discover that

1. There were, at the time, good and sufficient reasons for decisions that seem idiotic today.

2. The person most responsible is now your client, or your client's manager.

For these and other reasons, when you apply Boulding's Backward Basis, you should remember Sparks's Law of Problem Solution:

The chances of solving a problem decline the closer you get to finding out who was the cause of the problem.

Study Guides

In order to avoid the easy trap of placing blame, a consultant needs a few principles to guide the historical study. The first rule might be

Keep it simple and not too detailed; you're a consultant, not a district attorney.

If you interrogate people, you may offend them. Moreover, your questions may lead them in directions that they deem unimportant, while steering them around or away from what they think is important. You may not agree with their assessment of importance, but their priorities in and of themselves are always important facts. So ask less and listen more.

Of course, all this listening could fill your mind with trivia. To help you decide which details can be safely ignored,

Study for understanding, not for criticism.

Quite naturally, people who are responsible for the situation that is now considered a problem will be in a sensitive mood, for any proposed change could be interpreted as a slur on their character, intelligence, or foresight. They are likely to want to talk in order to explain their position, but if you sound critical, they will clam up.

The people who know the history are your best source of information. Rather than shut them up with criticism, try opening them up:

Look for what you like in the present situation, and comment on it.

The bad will come to the fore soon enough. If you don't mention it, other people surely will. Even the perpetrators themselves. Mrs. Oldenhauser knows how bad her white bread is today. After all, she's had her own history to study all these years. Just as your clients have. Just as you have. Haven't you?

THE WHY WHAMMY

If you have the knack of getting information that other people can't get, you'll never starve. Many of my clients hire me as a "mirror"—a tool for seeing themselves. But sometimes a client turns the tables on me, and gives me a view of myself that I couldn't even see in a mirror. Like Lambert, at the Seventh National Bank.

How to Dress a Consultant

It started out innocently enough as a day spent giving Seventh National a general checkup. The next morning, I was expected to provide a few fresh insights, for which I was to receive a fabulous fee. My plan was to spend a quiet dinner reviewing my notes and generating ideas for the morrow.

When Lambert volunteered to drive me to the hotel, he looked like a twelve-year-old in a three-piece suit, trying to look like a banker. Here was an obvious chance to apply The Inverse Gilded Rule. Lambert was gilding himself to look like something he wasn't, which meant he had something to hide. I should have known better than to accept the ride. Whenever I disregard that look of wide-eyed innocence, I get myself into hot water.

It seems that Lambert was playing taxi because he had a personal question, one that he dared not ask at the bank. We were waiting for the elevator when he blurted it out: "Why do you dress like that?" he asked, pointing with five fingers and not blinking his eyes.

I wasn't prepared, but I parried for time. "Like *what?*"

"Like you do. No suit. No tie. Jeans."

"They're *dress* jeans," I mumbled defensively.

"Well, then, *why* are they dress jeans, and not blue jeans? And why don't they cover your socks? And those tan shoes! Why not dark brown? or black? Here you are, working in a bank . . . "

"I'm only *consulting* in the bank. *You* work in the bank."

" . . . consulting in a bank, . . . but you look like you're dressing for a picnic, or something."

"What's wrong with dressing for a picnic?"

"Nothing. Don't get me wrong; I'm not criticizing you. I just want to know why you dress that way. I always thought I had to dress for the job, but you seem to be able to get away with dressing for a picnic. I'd like to understand, that's all. Maybe I'm dressing the wrong way."

He was so sincere I stopped being offended. "Listen, Lambert, I've arrived at this way of dressing after many years. I don't think I could explain it to you in a few minutes."

"That's all right. I just thought you might have a simple answer. Maybe if I let you think about it, you can tell me something helpful tomorrow."

"Okay," I said. "Maybe tomorrow."

Back at the hotel, I could barely get the question off my mind long enough to order supper. Rather than reviewing my notes, I sunk into a morass of introspection. Why *did* I dress this way?

It wasn't that I couldn't think of any reasons. My mind was filled with things I could tell Lambert. For one thing, it was important to me to be comfortable, so I could keep my mind on my consulting assignment. For another, I was traveling, and certain clothes pack significantly better than others. Then, too, I was not visiting just the bank on this trip. I had two other client sites to visit, at one of which I'd never seen a string tie, let alone a cravat, and the other in a city that was warmer and wetter than this one. I had to be prepared for anything.

Another factor was that I hadn't consulted at Seventh National before. I didn't know the culture, so I had to guess at what they'd be wearing and at what they'd find acceptable on me. I was working with people at several levels, some professional and some managerial, and I didn't want to be identified too closely with either group. Otherwise, one side might not open up to me, or listen to what I had to say.

I had to admit there were some less logical factors, too. There were current styles, which no doubt had at least a subliminal influence. There was ignorance: I know so little about fashion that I could be in and out and back in again without realizing it. Like a stopped clock that's right twice a day, I'm bound to be in fashion once in a while if I stick to the same old wardrobe.

Maybe not. I imagine that some of my outfits were *never* in fashion, and never will be. I wear my pants short because I have short legs for my size, and as a kid, my ready-to-wear pants were always too long. The other kids laughed when I rolled up the cuffs. But if I didn't roll them, I caught hell from my mother for coming home dipped in mud.

Scratching my head to think of other factors, I remembered my allergies. I can't wear wool or synthetics next to my body, and if anything metal touches me, my skin bubbles like boiling taffy. Without wool, it's hard to keep warm enough, so I wear several layers. I can wear a wool sweater, but only if I wear a cotton turtleneck underneath to keep it from touching my epidermis.

Of course, it could be that I wear the turtleneck because I hate ties with an irrational passion. I read once that the word "cravat" comes from the French word for Croatian, after the style of Louis XIV's Croatian soldiers. That made sense to me, because the word "slave" comes from the word "Slav," or Serbo-Croatian. To me, anyone wearing a tie looks like he has a rope around his neck.

I must admit that this prejudice saves me a lot of money. I am considered careful with money, which may have a lot to do with my failure to keep up with fashion in shirts, pants, coats, shoes, and even socks.

Yes, even socks. At least there I don't have a chance to make the wrong choice, because I only have one kind of socks, and they're all the same color. I buy them thirty pairs at a time, because I fold the laundry in our house, and because I can't stand trying to match socks. Having them all the same lets me choose socks in the dark, without waking up Dani, when I'm off to catch an early flight.

But the biggest reason for the socks is the money. If the hotel laundry tears or loses one sock, I don't have to throw away the other one. I guess I could get the laundries to reimburse me—they sure charge enough—but I can't abide the hassle. I go to great lengths to keep my life hassle-free.

I'd even buy special clothes if my client required it. Right now, I don't own a tie, but if it were important to my client, I'd purchase one and put it on my bill. . . . My bill! My client! What was I doing here, perseverating about clothes? I had work to do!

But it was too late. I'd wasted so much time, I had no time to work on Seventh National's problems. My only hope was to get enough sleep to be sharp in the morning. As I tossed and turned, with visions of unmatched socks dancing in my head, I cursed Lambert and his damned question.

In the morning, the curse was still on my lips. To me, Lambert was like the grasshopper who innocently asked the centipede, "When you take a walk, how do you decide which leg to move first?" I was like that wretched centipede who never took another step.

The Endless Supply of Reasons

Lambert, in his wide-eyed systems analysis innocence, had put me under The Why Whammy. I should have known better. My father always warned me:

We may run out of energy, or air, or water, or food, but we'll never run out of reasons.

People can give reasons for why they do things, and if you're not satisfied, they can give you more reasons. And more. And more again.

People can do just as well with reasons for why *not*. Or, like Hamlet, with reasons on both sides at the same time.

Lambert had hooked me with a "why" question, and I had tried to answer it in a finite amount of time. As a result, I was going into the bank unprepared, and I was going to lose the business.

But wait! If Lambert could Why Whammy me, perhaps I could Why Whammy him and his colleagues. Gathering confidence, I strode into the bank and began asking questions about yesterday's information.

"Why is your system built this way?"
"Why is the change needed by July 1?"
"Why do you run your organization like this?"
"Why don't you use that machine more?"
"Why do you use this machine so much?"
"Why does your form request this information?"
"Why doesn't it request this other information?"

It worked. They talked. They argued. They poured out information, far more in fact than I had gathered during the entire previous day.

By the end of the day, they were so impressed with my powers of observation that I had a contract to come back for three more days of consulting. And I was so pleased with *myself* that I was ready to accept Lambert's offer to take me to the airport.

Sure enough, before we were on the freeway, Lambert raised the clothing question. This time, though, I was ready. "Why *not* dress this way, Lambert. You can't run around naked, so you have to dress some way. Why not *this* way?"

Unfortunately, Lambert was too much the innocent systems analyst to fall for that one. "And *why* can't you run around naked?" he asked.

I'll forever be thankful to the unknown driver of a green 1975 Valiant who just then swerved in front of Lambert's Cougar, giving me time to shake off The Why Whammy. By the time Lambert had recovered his composure, I was ready.

"Really, Jerry, if you can dress any way you want, why can't you run around naked?"

"You see, Lambert," I said as he turned off the freeway and onto the airport entrance ramp, "if God had intended us to run around naked, we would have been *born* naked."

I heard no more whammies from Lambert, and completed the trip without further difficulties.

SEEING BEYOND THE CONSPICUOUS

The Bigness Is Not the Horse

Giving your clients The Why Whammy is an excellent way to get facts, but that still leaves you with the problem of seeing the principles underlying the facts. An even more powerful technique is to learn a principle from a client, then apply the principle to that client's problem. Rick is a data processing manager, but his first love is training horses. He recently came to Lincoln to work on his company's maintenance problems, but before we started to work, he insisted that we visit the horse show at the Nebraska State Fair.

Although I trained my German shepherd Sweetheart, large animals like horses have always been a mystery to me. In fact, when I'm around horses, all I can think of is what would happen if one of them stepped on my foot. When I mentioned my fears to Rick, he chuckled and said, "The bigness is not the horse."

"What does that mean?" I asked.

"Why don't you think about it for a while," he said. "That's what you always tell me to do with your mysterious consulting advice."

I had no choice but to shut up and watch the horses, but I didn't get it at all. When we returned to my office, Sweetheart greeted Rick at the door. He stood frozen on the threshold. "What's wrong?" I asked.

He gestured fearfully toward Sweetheart. "Look at those teeth. She could eat me alive!"

The Label Law

I laughed and showed him how he could see from her posture and the way she wagged her tail that she wasn't about to bite him. In fact, his only danger was that she might lick his hand.

"Okay," Rick said, cautiously extending his hand for a tongue bath. "I believe you. You see, it's just what I meant when I said, 'The bigness is not the horse.' Horse trainers working with a horse notice dozens of important characteristics, weighing each one for its possible importance in the training. To people who don't train horses, the only thing they notice is the first and most obvious thing: their size."

Rick had given me a lesson in what I now call The Label Law:

Most of us buy the label, not the merchandise.

Linguists and philosophers put this in a different way:

The name of a thing is not the thing.

In this way, they remind us of our tendency to attach a name—a label—to every new thing we see, and then to treat that thing as if the label were a true and total description. Even though Rick knew The Label Law, he was a horse trainer, not a dog trainer. All *he* could notice about Sweetheart was her teeth.

The true expert can see multiple aspects of a situation, but the novice sees only bigness, or teeth, or whatever is most conspicuous. Eskimos have dozens of words for snow, and Eskimos can actually see dozens of different kinds of snow. We Southerners see one, which we call "snow." But as we learn to ski, we expand our snow vocabulary to rival the Eskimo's, with such terms as "deep powder" and "corn snow." Learning to speak with more precision about snow, we learn to solve skiing problems more effectively.

It's the same with any consulting problem. The incompetent consultant doesn't define problems, but simply *labels* them with the first word that comes to mind. It might be a gilded label supplied by a client who's trying to hide something, or it simply could be a label describing the most conspicuous aspect of the situation. And once the stereotyped label is firmly attached, the problem becomes much harder to solve.

Maintenance Versus Design

During the past few years, I've received an increasing number of calls, in addition to the call from Rick, requesting me to help reduce the cost of software maintenance. I'm learning that the word "maintenance" is one of the poorest labels we've ever invented.

Rick started our session by saying that he spent eighty percent of his software budget doing maintenance. I suggested that perhaps this large amount merely meant that he was lumping too many things under one label, the way I had looked at horses and seen only their massive size. He agreed to let me look at some of the actual work done under the maintenance label.

I tried to look at the work the way an Eskimo looks at snow. I found that roughly half the work ought to have been labeled differently. For instance, prices which changed every few months were built right into the programs, rather than stored in easily maintained and checked tables. A team of three programmers spent its full time updating prices by changing the software.

The choice of terms had influenced the way Rick tried to improve the situation. By calling this work maintenance, Rick had directed attention to the efficiency of this team's coding and testing. I suggested that he speak of this problem as a "mismatch between design approach and maintenance abilities."

Seen from this perspective, the problem could be attacked either as a design problem or as a maintenance problem. The team of programmers decided to redesign the code using a table of prices—a table that already was maintained by the user department. The team's "maintenance" work simply disappeared. As an extra benefit, the user was thrilled to have his tedious job of maintaining the price list put on a microcomputer word processor.

The Misdirection Method

One of my clients told me the story of the optimist and the pessimist who were arguing about philosophy. The optimist declares, "This is the best of all possible worlds." The pessimist sighs and says, "You're right."

This story is representative of many long-lasting conflicts that can be traced to two parties labeling the same situation differently, even when they use the same words. In a surprising number of situations, the labeling is not only different, but actually complementary. This same client told me that his big problem was overrunning the budget on all development projects. When I visited the programmers, however, they told me that management was stingy with resources, never giving them enough to do the job properly. The same situation the manager called overrun, the programmers called underbudgeted.

Attaching an emotionally charged label to direct attention away from one aspect of a situation is called The Misdirection Method. Labeling the situation as an overrun assumes that the budget was correct. Labeling it as underfunding assumes that the work was done as efficiently as possible. Each label tends to steer people away from examining one aspect of the project. Managers, who make budgets, tend to speak of overruns, because that protects them from looking at their contribution to the problem. Workers, who don't make budgets, tend to speak of underfunding, because that throws attention off them and onto management.

The Three-Finger Rule

No consultant should be fooled by a client's attempts at misdirection, but it's something that happens to all of us. One of the most effective ways to catch yourself being misled is to look for the pointed index finger. Many people unconsciously reinforce their attempt to misdirect you by waving or pointing their index finger. Whenever I see this finger in the air, I remind myself of the Chinese Proverb:

When you point a finger at someone, notice where the other three fingers are pointing.

This even helps when *I'm* the one pointing the finger of misdirection.

THE FIVE-MINUTE RULE

In the final analysis, only the inexperienced consultant is worried about gathering facts. There are so many ways to improve your vision that the experienced consultant knows that facts will never be in short supply. Indeed, when I first enter a new consulting assignment, my biggest problem is the overwhelming flood of facts . . . long, boring stories from everyone I interview . . . thousands of reasons why this and not that . . . name-calling and finger-pointing. Over the years, I've become convinced that somewhere in that mass of facts is the solution to the client's problems, a solution that the clients themselves could see if it weren't for the overwhelming flood.

But they are overwhelmed, so they call in a consultant, who listens to what they say and spins it back in a slightly different package. Nowadays, the primary method I use for reducing the flood of facts is The Five-Minute Rule:

Clients always know how to solve their problems, and always tell the solution in the first five minutes.

This was true of Wilfram, whose problem of creeping change was woven into the white bread story he told Sparks. It was true at the Seventh National Bank, where the problem eventually turned out to be excessive formality—in dress and in other areas—that was stifling everyone's creativity. It was true of Rick, who had mislabeled design problems as maintenance problems, as well as of the other client who couldn't distinguish between overrun and under budget.

As a consultant, I could have picked up these signals in the first five minutes, saving myself days of tedious fact-gathering, or at least giving myself a strong clue as to how to organize the facts. But sometimes I'm so afraid of the client and so nervous in the first few minutes that I don't listen carefully enough. All I do is look at the teeth.

5

seeing what's not there

Words are often useful, but it always pays to listen
to the music (especially your own internal music).
—Brown's Brilliant Bequest

I was so proud of "my" pin technique that for many years I used it every time I was called in to solve quality problems. But because the tool seemed so effective, I missed the obvious. One day I was visiting a new client about a different type of problem and noticed a pinboard for complaints.

"Oh," I said, pointing to the board, "are you having quality problems with your software?"

"No. Our software quality is the best in the business. Why do you ask?"

MISSING TOOLS

Then, I realized what I should have noticed long ago: The *absence* of some tool for tabulating complaints was a sign of quality problems. Tabulating complaints is part of the process of producing quality software. If that part of the process is missing, then it is pretty hard for people to know they are producing poor quality, and thus quite difficult for them to do anything about it. At all those other client sites, once I'd introduced tabulation I probably wouldn't have needed to do anything else. The feedback would have eventually led to changes in quality.

I was a bit embarrassed to discover that other people had invented my technique, and needed something to boost my image as a consultant. I prided myself on my ability to use the pinboard information to locate the group producing the worst quality. Then, I would help improve that group's quality by pointing out all the things it was doing wrong. This approach definitely improved quality, but I never felt quite right about the process. It almost seemed like I was practicing voodoo, sticking pins in the poor people who weren't doing a good job.

When you're not terribly smart, it helps to be a good listener. Eventually, I was asked, "Why are you so negative? Don't you want to see what our good programmers are doing?" Eureka! I had used the pins to focus on the products that were having quality problems, but I could just as well have used the technique to see which groups *weren't* having quality problems. When I visited those groups, I immediately learned a dozen new ways to improve software quality.

Once again, I had failed to notice what wasn't there. I was so problem-oriented, that I missed the non-problems, those problems that

71

might have been there but weren't. I took a long, searching look at my consultant's tool kit and concluded that I was missing the tools I needed to see what wasn't there. I still haven't found all those missing tools, but now I do have a couple that I never had before. If only I could see which ones are still missing. . . .

REASONING FROM WHAT ISN'T THERE

Young consultants tend to be rather proud of their own ideas. It really punctured my balloon to discover that others had invented the pinboard technique long before I was born. As I became wiser, I learned that there are few new tools, although there are new ways to use old tools.

When I first thought of the pinboard technique, I didn't make full use of it. The pinboard doesn't simply tell which problems are present or absent, but it also reveals which ones are causing how much trouble. Once you know that, you can apply Boulding's Backward Basis to find out a lot about the system that produced the particular problem distribution.

The Level Law

For instance, if you apply Rudy's Rutabaga Rule several times, you will affect the distribution of your remaining problems. Suppose that out of every 1,000 complaints about your product line, the three biggest problems produce 700, 150, and 60 complaints, respectively, with 90 complaints for all the other products taken together. If you could completely eliminate the problems in the worst product, which is causing 70 percent of your complaints, the remaining products will have a distribution of 150, 60, and 90 for all the rest. If you then fix the next worst product, which accounts for 50 percent of the remaining complaints, you will be left with a product with 60 complaints and 90 complaints for all the rest, or only 40 percent of all your troubles for your biggest problem.

Little by little, as you keep solving your worst problem, the percent of trouble caused by your worst problem will diminish, and your remaining problems will tend to become relatively equal in percentage. That's why The Level Law holds:

Effective problem-solvers may have many problems, but rarely have a single, dominant problem.

To the extent that The Level Law holds true, a consultant can learn quite a bit about a client by observing the distribution of trouble across the existing problems. If you as a consultant find a relatively even distribution of problems, you may hypothesize that your clients are not seeing one major problem, but it is more likely that they have been keeping up with their problems without letting any one problem get out of control.

The fact that no one major problem exists implies that some effective problem-solving mechanisms are already in place. Even though you may not solve any spectacular problem, you can identify the client's favorite problem-solving mechanisms in order to use them in your own suggested methods. This should make you look good to the client.

The Missing Solution

When a client has one preponderant problem, it suggests that the client is missing something even more important—solution methods and/or strategies for ranking the severity of the problems. To understand why this follows, apply Boulding's Backward Basis. If one problem accounts for a major part of all the trouble, and has done so for some time, the client is evidently not terribly effective at problem-solving and has not been concentrating on problems in a worst-first manner.

Although the payoff for a solution to the worst problem would be big, the consultant in this situation is not likely to find a very fertile environment for ideas to take root. Instead of looking for existing problem-solving mechanisms, you may want to do something simple that will knock out a visible chunk of the big problem and do it in such a way as to increase your credibility. You can then use your credibility to gain a commitment of some resources to start on the next chunk.

But the drawback of this strategy is that it makes the clients more dependent on the consultant, and thus even less able to solve their own problems. A better approach may be to ignore the big problem initially and work to establish the clients' own problem-solving mechanisms. Choose something simple and relatively certain of success. Even though the solution of a minor problem has a low payoff in and of itself, the clients will learn how to solve their own problems themselves. An added benefit is that they will gain needed confidence.

The Missing History

It's important to look not only at the distribution of problems, but the history of that distribution. If the preponderant problem is something recent, perhaps introduced by some sudden external event, it's probably a good strategy to attack the problem directly, mobilizing the problem-solving mechanisms that the client already possessed before the new problem exploded onto the scene.

For instance, at one of my clients, a key designer was thrown from her horse and killed. I knew from my earlier consulting that this was a healthy organization, where key people regularly took vacations while others somehow coped during their absence. Rather than suddenly hire a replacement or promote an inexperienced designer, we established a plan to have each of the remaining staff designers take over a portion of the deceased designer's work, generally one with which they were moderately familiar. At the same time, they were allowed to choose some aspects of their own work that they could most easily transfer to less experienced people.

This careful allocation of tasks enabled the client to deal with what otherwise could have been a crippling setback. But for an organization at which everyone defers vacations and works overtime, and nobody knows what anyone else is doing, this would have been precisely the wrong approach. Such an organization would be hit hard by a sudden departure—although ironically, such an organization is most likely to experience sudden departures. If I were called upon to consult in such a situation, I would try to use the organization's present fears of disaster to motivate it to make some small but significant structural changes, such as a system of design reviews where people could become more familiar with each other's work.

The Missing Request for Help

Given the nature of clients, I would probably be asked for some quick solution to the immediate problem, but no quick solution would be likely to help much. Generally, though, I don't have to face this problem, because people who are so poor at solving problems very seldom ask for outside help. What's missing there is the request for help. Keep that in mind when you happen to be around and some problem suddenly surfaces. Because you are a consultant, you may find yourself implicitly involved in searching for a solution, but implicit involvement isn't good enough. Make sure that you've actually been asked.

It's one of the ironies of our business that consultants rarely get asked for help by the people who need help the most. That sometimes makes it tempting to jump in without being asked when you happen to be in the neighborhood. Don't! When the request is missing, chances are you can't help.

Some consultants have clients who are forced to see them, somewhat like delinquent kids who are forced to see a court-appointed psychiatrist. If you're having trouble finding clients, you may envy such consultants, but you probably couldn't live with their discouraging success rate. Such consultants quickly learn that their first agenda item is to get the client to supply the missing request for help. Even at that task, they generally don't succeed.

HOW TO SEE WHAT ISN'T THERE

Acting on the absence of a request for help is but one example of how a consultant uses *missing* elements as a guide to action. Other actions might be triggered when the consultant notices, for example, that there are no women in an organization or no people between the ages of 35 and 50, that the project leader shows no regret when talking about people who have left, or that nobody ever talks about the training department. I was helped in one assignment when I noticed that there were no visible personal items in anyone's office. In a second, nobody used certain features of a new computer. In a third, I got off to a good start when I realized that a project's delivery date was never mentioned. Examples such as these have convinced me that I should cultivate the ability to notice missing things—to see what *isn't* there.

But how can I see what isn't there? I don't have any final answers, but I can give you some approaches I've found helpful.

Be Aware of Your Own Limitations

Because every consulting situation is different, it's hard to give general rules about what's missing. But there's one thing that's *not* missing in every single one of your consulting situations: you. Suppose you missed X, Y, and Z in your previous assignment. Apply Boulding's Backward Basis and ask why? The answer is probably that *you* personally are missing something, namely, the power to observe X, Y, and Z. And so, unless you do something about this missing power of observation, you'll probably miss X, Y, and Z again on your next assignment.

In my case, I've always had a problem noticing that nobody asked me for help in the first place, and so I've developed techniques that *force* me to notice. When prospective clients call, I always ask them to confirm their call in a simple letter. I can study a letter more easily than a verbal request, to see what they really have and have not asked me to do.

Even when I'm visiting a client and am asked to do something on the spot, I ask that the request be put in writing. If I must respond immediately, I write my understanding of the request in my notebook and ask the client to read and approve it. Most of the time, I haven't heard the request correctly, so writing and checking prevents trouble.

Although I find this a valuable technique, it may prove worthless to you or even offensive to your clients. I'm not recommending any specific technique, but a general technique that says

> Find out what you usually miss and design a tool to ensure that you don't miss it again.

Use Other People

The diversity of people can frustrate any consultant because he or she must assess the individual characteristics of each new environment, but when it comes to seeing what's missing, diversity is your ally. Pose the question "What am I missing?" to as many people as you can find. Approach insiders for their long familiarity with the situation. Use outsiders for the fresh, naive view. Recruit people at different levels, with different roles, and with different backgrounds. Listen to their first impressions, but also allow the question to simmer in their minds.

In one organization, I worked with a group on the task of increasing programmer productivity. I tried to discover whether group members were missing any useful tools that might have enhanced productivity, but that seemed not to be the case since the policy was to purchase or build anything any programmer requested.

I wasn't getting anywhere, so I called a break. While walking to the men's room, I stopped to ask the janitor what was missing in the organization. He thought for a moment and then said, "They never let me wash their blackboards." That struck a chord, and I sampled the offices: Every one had a full board with a SAVE sign more or less permanently displayed.

When I returned to the meeting, I raised the question of the use of the blackboards, which in turn raised the larger question of the proper use of other tools. Properly used, a blackboard can be a social tool for stimulating ideas, but it doesn't serve that purpose when it's used as a permanent, private bulletin board, full of essential telephone numbers and computer codes that can never be erased. The discussion revealed that the group was not missing any conceivable tool, but was missing procedures that would have ensured effective *use* of the tools. Most of the tools were as poorly used as the blackboards, a situation we set out to remedy.

Investigate Other Cultures

The janitor example suggests another "What's missing?" technique. The janitor lives in a different subculture from the programmers, and thus sees things that are invisible to them. If we can find other subcultures, we can use them as models to be compared with the culture under investigation. As a consultant, I see many different organizations, each of which has some ways of doing things that are missing in others. I make a particular effort to get consulting assignments outside the United States, because they open my eyes to what's missing in my own culture, as well as to things I've always taken for granted.

In Denmark, for instance, many small firms retain a "lunch lady" to bring in a most attractive sandwich buffet every day. An entire working group will sit down to lunch together. It's a jovial time, but one in which participants make many important decisions about matters of mutual interest. When conducting problem-solving sessions, we noticed that whenever Danes had a decision to make, they would get around a large table and share some kind of food or drink, thus recreating a familiar decision-making environment.

Some American work groups have evolved a similar practice, but many others seem to fly apart whenever there is a break for food or drink. After my experience in Denmark, I'm able to see this typically American practice as missing an opportunity to develop group decision-making skills. In several firms, I've convinced the management to subsidize one really nice group lunch each week, which generally pays off in improved teamwork.

Use Laundry Lists

Rather than rely on your memory of other situations, it's sometimes useful to develop explicit lists of items that may be missing. In our work on technical reviews, we developed a number of lists, such as of materials you might want in your meetings, steps to be taken in preparing for reviews, or of points to look for in a reviewed document. We called them checklists until one of our clients pointed out that they were more like laundry lists. A laundry list reminds you of the different items that you might have forgotten, but that just might need cleaning up. A checklist is similar, but says these are items that *must* be present. The list of ideas you're now reading is a laundry list, not a checklist. You don't have to do every one of these things, but you might want to consider them.

When working in poorly defined situations, you probably can't say in advance what elements *must* be present for success, so a laundry list is preferred. It's also important not to get too confident about your list, lest you become even more likely to miss something critical.

Check the Process

In addition to telling you *what's* missing, a laundry list can be used in another way. It can be used to determine whether your search for missing things has been effective. Keep your laundry list in reserve until after you have your own list of missing items. Then compare the two lists. If the laundry list brings up new items, perhaps your original process of thinking up missing items wasn't that comprehensive. Try changing the process in some way and continue working.

Although a good process won't ensure that you see everything, a poor process will almost certainly cause you to overlook something. Any indication that your process was poor is an indication that a new process should be fruitful. When working with an organization, I may conduct a meeting to identify missing items. If a meeting is dominated by one or two individuals, I know that I'm not getting the ideas of all the others. I try to keep the dominant individuals under control, but if I can't, I terminate the meeting. Then I meet the participants individually in an environment more conducive to their participation.

ON BEING RIDICULOUS

So, what's missing from *this* laundry list of techniques for seeing what's missing? I checked it against itself, and it seemed quite reasonable, which is exactly what's wrong with it! If I don't come up with a few unreasonable items, then the process has been too conservative.

When I was young and confused, I looked forward to being older and wiser, or at least to having solid lists of reliable ideas that would make me look wise. But now that I'm old enough to be acquainted with the conservative realities of life, I can't cope with the farfetched speculations of the young.

Why I Stopped Being a Professor

A few years back, I thought I had grown wise enough to be a college professor. I treasured that illusion for a few weeks—that is, until I came in contact with the students. From then on, it was all downhill. I did struggle for a long time, even presuming to teach a course in systems thinking—as if I had anything to teach. It was the systems thinking class that delivered the coup de grâce to my professorial tenure.

Judy had lingered after class to tell me she was transferring to Oberlin College. Judy's quick, teasing wit marked her as someone exceptional, so I was disappointed to be losing her as a disciple.

"It's not so much the school," she comforted me. "My sister goes to Oberlin, and we're very close."

"Is she an older sister or a younger sister?"

"Neither."

"Neither?"

"We were born on the same day."

"Aha," I triumphed. As co-discoverer of Weinbergs' Law of Twins, I was now on familiar ground. "You're twins!"

"No, we're not twins."

"Born on the same day, but you're not twins? Are you step-sisters?"

"No, we have the same parents."

"Then you're adopted!"

"No, we have the same *biological* parents."

"Hmmnh. Born to the same parents, on the same day, and not twins? I'll have to think about that. What am I missing?"

"Think about it. Let's see you apply some of the principles you've been teaching us."

I'll spare you the agonies I endured rather than say the dreaded words, "I don't know. Tell me." By the time the next class rolled around, my eyes were almost as baggy as my trousers.

Apparently Judy had seen the symptoms before. As a pre-med, she couldn't stand the sight of human suffering, so she came up and spoke without forcing me to admit defeat.

"Triplets," she said, and my ego bubble burst. My mind raced through a thousand reasons why the riddle wasn't fair. It would just never do to be bested by this little snippet of a girl. She might lose all respect for higher education. She might behave badly at Oberlin. What would they think of us, sending them such an impertinent student?

"Don't you think that's a little farfetched?" It was the best I could concoct, but I needed time to rationalize.

"How can it be farfetched, Jerry, when I actually am one of triplets?"

I should have listened to those other professors. They warned me that letting students use my first name would soon lead to other liberties. And even worse, there were *other* students watching. Perhaps I could play their sympathies to my advantage.

"Naturally it doesn't seem farfetched to *you*, but how many of the people here have ever met a triplet before?" I held my breath. No, I had guessed right. None of them knew triplets. "See, it *is* rather farfetched, at least in that sense of the word."

That should have taught her not to get into semantic arguments with professors, but youth is not wise enough to admit defeat. "I can't accept that reasoning," she continued. "It could be that you've never before met any sisters who weren't twins even though they were born on the same day. But it could also be that you've conveniently forgotten, just to prove your point."

"I certainly wouldn't forget sisters like that, if I'd ever known any."

"I think you would. In fact, I think I can *prove* that you would. How about a little wager? Would you be willing to put five dollars on it?"

Now I know that no honorable professor would take money from a poor student. But Judy needed a lesson she would remember once she got to Oberlin, otherwise she'd get in a lot of trouble with professors who weren't as broad-minded as I am. "Okay, you're on. And these are our witnesses when the bet is finally settled."

"Oh, that won't take long. We can settle it right now."

"Right now? How can you possibly prove I've met sisters born on the same day to the same parents who weren't twins?"

"Because you've got two such sisters living in your own house!"

"What? In my own house? Don't be ridi—. Arrrgh!"

That was the sound of the air escaping from my over-inflated windbag. At that moment, I decided that laughing at myself was a great deal more fun than being a professor. Besides, I couldn't help myself.

Weinberg's Law of Fetch

I told the story about fifty times that day (even a retiring professor has *some* privileges). When I arrived home, I just couldn't resist telling Dani. I also told the two sisters, born to the same parents, on the same day, who are not twins.

Although they probably didn't fully appreciate the story, Rose and Sweetheart love to bark and wag their tails when they hear us laughing, so they joined in the fun. Because they hear better than they see, and because "fetch" is their favorite game, I composed Weinberg's Law of Fetch:

Sometimes farfetched is only shortsighted.

I did want to call it Weinberg's Law of Triplets, but that would have spoiled the riddle. Besides, Rose and Sweetheart aren't triplets. I believe there were seven in their litter.

The Rule of Three

I suppose I'm not the only one who wants to be smart and successful, and who thereby sets himself up to lose bets and look foolish. Wanting to be right all the time makes it especially difficult to notice what's missing in your own thought processes. After losing that embarrassing bet to Judy, however, I decided that I'd have to enlarge my repertoire of "What's missing?" skills, especially with techniques that could be applied to my own thinking.

From my work with software designers, I already had discovered one such "What's missing?" tool that I could have applied to solve Judy's riddle, but I didn't recognize it out of context. As a check on the software design process, we teach The Rule of Three:

> **If you can't think of three things that might go wrong with your plans, then there's something wrong with your thinking.**

The Rule of Three can be used to check any thinking process. It invariably turns up something that everybody missed, and if you're a bettor, it will save you lots of money on "sure things."

LOOSENING UP YOUR THINKING

The first time you apply The Rule of Three, though, you'll probably find people complaining, "But I can't think of anything else." For times like these, every consultant should have a repertoire of idea-generating techniques, such as brainstorming, brainwriting, and games. Here are some of the ones we use.

Look for Analogies

Think of some system that is somehow like the one you're examining, then use it as a source of ideas. Biology, psychology, engineering, sports, family life, health—they're all candidates. It's not necessary for the systems to be identical; you're looking for ideas, not answers.

In one organization, we were studying their technical training program when someone suggested the analogy of animal training. This analogy made us realize that we'd been concentrating on the *content* of training, rather than the implicit system of reward and punishment. This led to a small survey of recent trainees, which showed that many of them regarded the video training as a form of punishment, because they had to sit alone in a poorly ventilated, dirty stockroom when they viewed the tapes. The situation was easily corrected, resulting in a startling increase in the number of requests for training.

Move to Extremes

Another way to explore the unexplored is to take some attribute of the system and imagine what would happen if you moved it to some extreme value. What if costs doubled? What if we could get these parts for nothing? What if we could manufacture these items in zero gravity? What if all government regulations were suddenly removed? You don't expect these things to happen, but playing with them in your mind distorts the current system and lets you see things that were previously concealed by reasonableness.

For instance, in studying morale and turnover problems, we imagined what would happen to the organization if there were no turnover whatsoever. This led us to realize one of the previously unnoticed benefits of turnover: the influx of new ideas when new people were hired. As programs were implemented to reduce turnover, other programs were added to supplement the flow of new ideas to the organization.

Look Outside the Boundary

We all know that things tend to fall between cracks and that cracks occur at boundaries, where one system joins another. A computer system may have powerful diagnostic programs for finding trouble in each component, but when there is a problem with cables, for example, none of the special diagnostic programs seems to be able to find it. The boundary between one part of a system and another is a good place to look for missing things—those things that each part assumes are taken care of by the other part.

To look for these between-the-cracks items, first list all the edges of a system and all boundaries within the system, and then list all the activities that ought to transpire at those edges. People will object, saying "That's not part of the problem," but that's just a clue that you're on the right track. Using these lists as laundry lists often reveals overlooked items, like the customers who are left on hold because of a flaw in the procedures for switching incoming calls.

Look for Alibis Versus Explanations

Sam Spade, Miss Marple, and Charlie Chan all knew that any suspect with too elaborate an alibi must be guilty of something. Look for explanations and see if they are alibis for something that is missing. For example, on the tub of a hotel, we find a warning:

FOR YOUR SAFETY!
PLEASE NOTE BATHTUB ELEVATION.

Because this sign wasn't there on the previous visit, we suspect that it was added after someone fell getting out of the tub. The tub is mounted so its bottom is several inches above the floor level, which makes getting out very dangerous. The sign is there for safety, but even more it is there to protect the hotel from legal consequences the next time someone falls. In other words, it is there to protect the hotel from the consequences of forgetting to do it right in the first place.

When working with organizations, I often study their written standards and procedures in exactly the same way I study hotel signs. Buried in one procedures manual was a curious rule that prohibited the use of certain code combinations for identifying products. Tracing the history of this rule, I discovered that the programmers had used these codes for special internal records, a terrible programming practice that got them into trouble when someone accidentally assigned one of these internal codes.

Many written rules are instituted as quick fixes for problems that happened once in the past. The incident may be forgotten, but the rule lingers on as a clue to an event that may happen again. Prohibiting certain product codes did not solve the problem of this poor programming practice being used in other programs. When we searched the entire program library, we found a dozen other places that were vulnerable to the same kind of accident.

The Emotional Component

I'm still a bit surprised at how well "ridiculous" games reveal things we miss by more rational methods. I shouldn't be. Consultants rarely get called when the client's rational methods have been working well, so something different is always needed. One approach is to use a different rational method, but it may be more promising to be a bit irrational. This is hard to do, however, because when problems get difficult, everyone wants to be "rational."

The Incongruence Insight

Have you ever had a client stomp a foot, turn beet-red, and scream "BE RATIONAL!"? That kind of nonrational demand for rationality does tend to discourage me from making fresh suggestions, but it also reminds me that I may have been overlooking the emotional component of the problem.

A great turning point in my consulting life came when Nancy Brown, one of the world's great consultants, was observing me working with a client. I had just made a fantastic rational analysis of the client's problem, but it somehow felt all wrong. At a break, when I asked Nancy what I was missing, she said quietly, "Sometimes when I'm not getting anywhere with the words, I listen to the music." I wasn't exactly sure what she meant, but I resolved to try it after the break.

The client told me that his relationship with his co-workers was a great problem, but his voice and posture had been so relaxed that when I compared the words and the "music," I saw that his words made no sense. On the other hand, when my questions touched on his relationship with his boss, he started to fidget and his voice acquired a strained tone. Using this music as a clue, I quickly moved into an area I'd missed entirely, having been misled by his words which said, in effect, "Don't waste your time looking there." This led to a new definition of the problem as well as several new solution ideas.

What is missing in these cases is *congruence* between the words being used and the emotions being expressed. Over the years since that lesson, I've learned that the ability to sense incongruence is the consultant's most powerful "What's missing?" tool. I call this The Incongruence Insight:

When words and music don't go together, they point to a missing element.

The most effective method of finding that element is simply to comment on the incongruity and allow the client to respond. All I said to this client was, "I notice that your hands tremble while you talk about your wonderful relationship with your boss." I didn't try to interpret this incongruence, but merely brought it to his conscious attention. He looked startled for a moment, glanced down at his hands as if to confirm what I said, and then opened up to me about how he feared his boss so much that he was afraid to talk to anyone about it, lest there be repercussions.

BROWN'S BRILLIANT BEQUEST

Nancy also explained to me that listening to the music didn't apply just to the client. She pointed out that the reason I had asked her for help in the first place was that I had "felt" something was wrong with my analysis. Those feelings are part of the music, too—probably the most important part. The music you hear from the client is only the external sound of an internal emotional state that you cannot, of course, know directly.

But you can know your *own* emotional state directly, and your own emotional state tends to be quite sensitive to the client's music. When you feel something strong going on inside yourself, capture it and start listening to the client's music for clues about its origin. Or, comment about it to the client. Many times, I've found myself becoming angry about some incident a client is describing despite the fact that the client is speaking in a passionless manner. When I mention that something about the story seems to be making *me* angry, the clients often drop their emotional cover and tell me how angry the incident made them.

This method is so effective at seeing what's missing that I've given it a name. In honor of Nancy Brown's generous gift, I call it Brown's Brilliant Bequest:

Words are often useful, but it always pays to listen to the music (especially your own internal music).

Which brings us full circle, back to knowing yourself, which is where all good consulting work originates. Being able to see what's missing in ourselves is the only possible way to keep us from looking more ridiculous than we really are.

6

avoiding
traps

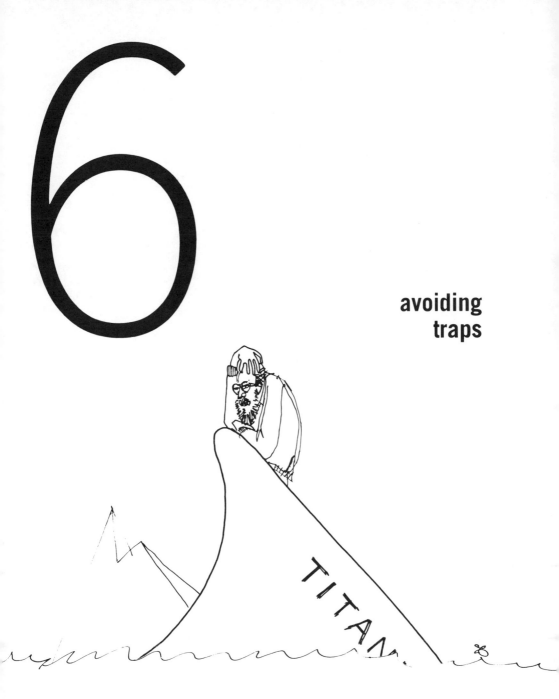

**The thought that disaster is impossible often leads
to an unthinkable disaster.**

—The Titanic Effect

When I was a green kid, I used to think I would write the Great American Novel, solve the Riddle of the Sphinx, and leap tall buildings in a single bound. As I grew older, I realized I wasn't going to accomplish these things; so I became a consultant who would tell other people how to accomplish them. I guess I thought that consultants, alone among the human race, could do something perfectly.

Little by little, I lowered my standards. Right now, in my private life, I'd be happy if I could write the Great American Sentence, solve the riddle of eating french fries without getting ketchup on my shirt, and step over a snowdrift without falling down and breaking my hip. In my consulting work, I'd be satisfied if I could just stay out of trouble.

STAYING OUT OF TROUBLE

I know now that *some* trouble cannot be avoided—such as a Soviet satellite that decides to penetrate your roof and make love to your television set—but that most of my troubles stem from the same source: me. That's why I've mastered The Bolden Rule, the technique of converting failure to feature. Even so, using The Bolden Rule may wear it out, or wear me out, so I've also studied the art of staying out of trouble.

Consultants are naturally eager to change the world, and I promise that later chapters will tell you exactly how to do that; but before you try leaping tall buildings in a single bound, you ought to know something about keeping your clients out of trouble—and about staying out of trouble yourself.

LAWS, RULES, AND EDICTS

A Mysterious Christmas Gift

I know Christmas is coming when I receive my free gift collection from Northern Natural Gas. Last year's package contained a calendar with a sepia print of "Evening Bivouac on the Missouri, 1834." This year it was "The Jury," depicting a fallen Indian warrior surrounded by a herd of buffalo.

The pictures change, but there's always a calendar. There's always a ball-point pen, too. And a phosphorescent key ring. And more.

Last year, there was a flexible magnet. Dani uses it to hang recipes on the refrigerator. This year, there was a plastic rain gauge. I appreciate that a rain gauge is more expensive than a flexible magnet, but I already have a rain gauge. Dani has hundreds of recipes, but we get only one rainfall at a time.

I thought of writing to Northern to complain, but I didn't want to seem ungrateful. After all, I hadn't the foggiest notion of why I was on their Christmas gift list in the first place. I don't even send them a card.

I mentioned the problem to Dani, thinking she might write the letter, seeing as how she is the one who uses the magnet. "Don't you think," she said, "that after seven years, it's about time you found out why they're sending us these presents?"

"That's part of the problem. What if they tell me it was a mistake, and I have to return the gifts? I've already used up three of the ball-point pens, and we gave away one of the key rings when we sold your car."

"Don't you have any clues?"

"What kind of clues?"

"Wasn't there ever a letter in the package?"

"Well, yes, I think there was. You don't suppose *that* would explain anything?"

"Aren't you the one who always tells me: 'When in doubt, read the instructions.'?"

Rather than answer the unanswerable, I slipped out and retrieved the crumpled letter. It opened with the customary Seasons Greetings, after which Northern thanked us effusively for letting them run their gas main through our property. Then, they expressed the hope that we would accept these humble tokens of their appreciation.

"How thoughtful," I said to myself, "but I could hardly tell them to *remove* the gas main, so why are they so solicitous of my good will? Business is business, at least to a big corporation like Northern. There *must* be more to it."

Then I noticed a sentence suggesting that if I ever happened to consider digging in the vicinity of their gas main, I might give them a call. The sentence was phrased so delicately, I had missed it on the first reading. Obviously, they didn't want to raise my anxiety about a potential natural gas disaster two hundred feet north of my house. But they *did* want me to think of them if I happened to head north with a shovel or bulldozer.

Of course. If *I* owned a gas pipeline, my nightmares would be filled with parades of farmers who lived along the line, each carrying a sharp shovel and driving a monster tractor.

How *do* you make people think gas? A letter? Not likely! Letters wind up crumpled in wastebaskets by the hundreds.

Back in the Forties, wherever you drove in the Midwest, you'd see a standard, red neon sign:

E AT   H E R E
G E T   G A S

Those signs all disappeared decades ago, but to this day, despite twenty thousand leagues over the Plains, whenever I see a restaurant with a red neon sign I think of getting gas. You might say my thoughts have been triggered.

Triggers

If I owned a pipeline, I would assemble the best experts money could buy. To this throng of experts, I would pose one problem: How can we remind the farmers to *think gas* whenever they are about to dig?

So, along with the letter, Northern Gas sends some *triggers*, each containing their phone number where it would likely be seen on the critical day. Finally, I understood the reasons behind the gifts:

- a calendar, to circle a date and write, "Dig today in the North Forty."
- a ball-point pen, to draw a digging map.
- a magnet, to hang the map on the refrigerator door.
- a rain gauge, to show if the ground is too wet to dig today.
- a key ring, to hold the key for the tractor, which could cost Northern a million dollars with one swipe of its blade.

I found Dani rearranging the recipes on the refrigerator. I told her I had discovered the reason for the gifts, but that I couldn't understand the magnitude of their concern. "Surely every farmer along the pipeline *knows* that the pipeline is there, and that it's dangerous to dig near it."

"Of course, they know. Just the way *you* know that if you want to understand what's in a package, you ought to read the letter that goes with it. If people only did what they know they ought to do, cars wouldn't need bumpers."*

---

*That's why I wrote this book of laws, rules, and edicts. They're like Northern's key ring. They plant triggers about things you *already* know, things you might forget just when you're about to start the tractor.

The Main Maxim

Whether I call a trigger a law, or a rule, or an edict, or a principle, the idea is the same. They're catchy phrases designed to pop into your mind when you're just about to do something you *know* you shouldn't do. Or to forget to do something you know you should do.*

For example, the law I discovered from Northern's Christmas packages I call The Main Maxim, with the pun on "main" intended:

What you don't know may not hurt you, but what you don't remember always does.

The pun works equally well for gas mains, water mains, and electric mains, which should delight your local utility company. But how can I make it explode in your mind next Christmas, when you start to assemble little Willie's bicycle before reading the instructions? Or next time you visit your most important client?

THE ART OF SETTING TRIGGERS

As a consultant, you need to be able to set triggers in your own head, and also in the heads of your clients. One of the most influential services you can provide is to help people stay out of trouble they know is there.

The Potato Chip Principle

Does the idea of triggers planted in your brain frighten you? It should. If you're like me, your head already contains several items you'd rather do without.

I know that my attic could use a good cleaning, but I've always been a little afraid of tampering with my mind. If I wasn't so afraid of what psychologists would find in my head, I would like to get some help. For one thing, I have a compulsion to eat potato chips.

---

*The name I use is designed to help you remember the trigger, whenever possible by puns, alliteration, or by some other device, as in Brown's Brilliant *Bequest*, Rudy's Rutabaga *Rule*, and Boulding's Backward *Basis*. The important thing is that you are triggered at the right moment, when you need the idea, rather than that you be able to list all rules, bequests, laws, and principles in some hierarchy. The most important law is the one you need right now, not the one I thought was most important when I named them.

But that's not the worst of it. I'm also a compulsive reader. I can't remember a time when I couldn't read, and from the very first, I read compulsively. Some of the earliest messages I remember reading were on potato chip boxes.

You'd think that after half a century I'd have learned all there was to know about potato chips, but I just caught myself doing it again:

> GUARANTEE: This product is manufactured to the highest quality standards. In the unlikely event that this product is not fresh or in good condition, return entire package top for replacement. *Print* your name and address and tell us why returned.

This message is printed in tiny letters at the bottom of the narrow side of the box. Don't they want me to notice it? No matter. For a compulsive reader and potato chip eater, *anything* written anywhere on a potato chip box, bag, or canister will pull the trigger. Which suggests The Potato Chip Principle:

If you know your audience, it's easy to set triggers.

Of course, it doesn't have to be potato chips. Subtle or blatant, printed material is all the same to me. The message on my phosphorescent key ring trumpets

> NORTHERN NATURAL GAS
> CALL US BEFORE YOU DIG OR BLAST

Ominous enough, and it glows in the dark. It will certainly trigger me, but will it work for you? When you're opening the dynamite locker at midnight, will you notice the glow? Or, will there be a gigantic pipeline explosion?

One-Liners

For the sane half of the human population, serious, written triggers aren't nearly as effective as funny ones spoken out loud. Will Rogers, the American humorist, was a master of the memorable one-liner. In fact, whenever I think of Will Rogers, I remember the line:

> "I never met a man I didn't like."

Which reminds me of a one-liner I read in 1974, on the wall of the men's room at Gumps in San Francisco:

"Will Rogers never met Richard Nixon."

Most of the time, compulsive readers immediately forget what they read, but that one-liner stuck. It made me realize I was growing older. In my youth, we didn't have Richard Nixon to kick around. There were no Richard Nixon jokes. There were Adolf Hitler jokes. We would have written,

"Will Rogers never met Adolf Hitler."

I remember reading a joke about Hitler's last days in his bunker:

The news from all fronts has turned sour. The Russians have reached Berlin. The Americans have crossed the Rhine and are racing to beat the Russians into Germany. Overwhelmed by this awful news, Hitler turns to his assembled staff and rants, "That's it! Enough is enough! From now on, *no more Mr. Nice Guy!*"

Now a line like that has got to be a good trigger for something important. Just now, though, it worries me that Will Rogers might have been right. Could it be that World War II was caused by a misunderstanding? Was poor Adolf really a kindly fellow, misunderstood by us all?

The Titanic Effect

There's always trouble when a national leader loses touch with public reality. The leader's power compounds the trouble, but that's not what makes a disaster. To quote Will Rogers again,

"It ain't what we don't know that gets us in trouble, it's what we know that ain't so."

I think Rogers was on to something big. I don't know about Hitler, but Nixon might have weathered the storm if he hadn't been so sure of himself. Ask any poker player who thought four aces was an unbeatable hand.

The rule in poker is that you don't lose your shirt on bad hands, but on hands that "can't lose." The owners of the *Titanic* "knew" that their ship was unsinkable. They weren't going to waste time steering around icebergs, or waste money having needless lifeboats.

This attitude can be devastating, as expressed in The Titanic Effect:

The thought that disaster is impossible often leads to an unthinkable disaster.

The trouble starts when you know something that "ain't so." Then, it gets worse because you are so aggressively sure of yourself that you act as if there's no *possibility* of being wrong. Because you're so sure of yourself, a minor mistake may be converted into a major tragedy.

Triggering on Natural Events

So how could we concoct a trigger for The Titanic Effect? If managers at Northern Natural Gas want to keep me from blasting their pipeline, they don't have to teach me exactly where the pipeline crosses my property. All they need to do is plant a seed of *uncertainty*. If you had the slightest doubt about where that pipeline was, would *you* light the fuse?

Of all the people in the world, the Swiss seem to have the best modern record of avoiding *Titanic*-like disasters. Can anyone conceive of a Swiss Hitler, or even a Swiss Nixon?

Now some will say that the famous Swiss democracy is the reason they stay out of trouble. Most Swiss don't even *know* who's President, so there's not much danger even from a President who happens to be a bit too self-confident.

But as a compulsive reader and potato chip muncher who lived in Switzerland for many years, I think I have a better answer: The Swiss have a secret trigger for The Titanic Effect.

There's a potato chip company in Switzerland with an enormous fleet of little red-and-yellow trucks scurrying through the streets. You can hardly walk a block in any city without a Zweifel truck zipping by. And if you happen to be a compulsive reader, that's all the trigger you need, for Zweifel in German means "doubt."

But if you aren't a compulsive reader, or aren't lucky enough to live in Appenzell or Zurich, what good does Zweifel do you? You'll need something else, something that happens all the time, like Zweifel trucks, to trigger a few healthy doubts about what you know for sure.

When you're playing poker, you might remember the *Titanic* whenever those tiny icebergs clink in your martini. In my case, I remember Will Rogers every time I meet a client I don't like. Then Will reminds me that what I know about that person may not be so.

BUILDING YOUR OWN BELL SYSTEM

It should now be quite clear to everybody that most of my troubles come not from falling satellites but from failing brain cells. My own. The Main Maxim cautions me:

What you don't know may not hurt you, but what you don't remember always does.

I know when I've had this kind of trouble when I mutter to myself: "You pea-brained idiot! You knew better than that." The Titanic Effect admonishes me:

The thought that disaster is impossible often leads to an unthinkable disaster.

I recognize Titanic Effects by their titanic effect, or when I swear under my breath: "You pigheaded fool! Can't you ever admit that you might be wrong?"

Knowing these things, I want to do something about them, but The White Bread Warning puts me on the alert:

If you use the same recipe, you get the same bread.

So what I need is a new recipe. I already know enough to stay out of Main Maxim trouble, but I need a new system of recipes to remind me when I'm about to do something when i should know better.

Knowing what I'm missing, where should I look for ideas? I was trying to think about this question, but the telephone kept ringing. After the third interruption—a wrong number—I swore out loud at myself, "Why can't I ignore this blasted bell!" I was sitting in front of a blank word processor screen, with an equally blank mind, when Dani came in.

"Why are you humming?" she asked.

"Humming? Was I humming?"

"I believe it was 'The Bells of St. Mary's.'"

"Eureka," I shouted. "Of course, the bells."

"Whatever are you raving about?"

"It's that bell. The telephone company designed that bell so cleverly that I wouldn't be able to ignore it, no matter what else I was doing. Without that feature, the telephone system wouldn't have succeeded."

"So?"

"So what I need is a bell system of my own." And that's what this chapter is about: how to build your own bell system, a system of triggers you simply *can't* ignore.

Attached Notes

Like the original Bell System, a personal bell system is built up step by step, and sometimes the old equipment impedes progress. Take the problem of restaurants. Some people have a problem eating in restaurants, but not me. My problem is *overeating* in restaurants. When I embark on a consulting trip, I'm usually so nervous about doing well that I stuff myself at the first opportunity. And then I feel so bad about overeating that I stuff myself on the whole trip, just to make me feel better.

I traced the problem back to a trigger my mother planted when I was four years old: "Whenever you don't feel well, eat something!" After forty-five years of indigestion, I fully understand that eating more to feel better doesn't work. But, as The Main Maxim says, it's forgetting that gives me indigestion.

Indigestion isn't even the worst part. Long after the trip is over, the problems forgotten, and the indigestion controlled, all those ugly pounds remain. To lose them, I read dozens of diet books, but not because reading burns more calories than running. Reading them makes me feel virtuous, and each is full of brilliant advice. Unfortunately, in the excitement of each new trip, I always forget the advice.

One of the books advised me that the next time I pigged out, I should think the following thoughts:

1. Remember that a lapse does not have to mean a relapse.

2. Resist negative thoughts.

3. Ask yourself what happened; then plan your strategy for next time.

4. Return to controlled eating immediately.

5. Talk to someone supportive.

6. Remember that you are making lifelong changes. You are not on a diet. Look at the progress you've made, and go to it.

I decided these thoughts had to be true because I'd seen them in at least three other books, although I would never remember them at the right time. I didn't need these thoughts when I was reading a diet book, but when I was eating in a restaurant.

Applying The Main Maxim, I typed the six thoughts on the back of a business card that I slipped into my wallet next to my American Express Card. Because I never pay cash when traveling, I would be sure to see the card at precisely the right moment, when I had just stuffed myself like a Strasbourg goose.

Does it work? Yes, much of the time. Now, when I come back from a two-week trip, I've gained only one or two pounds, rather than five or ten. As a result, I can occasionally afford the luxury of stuffing myself at home. Unfortunately, Dani doesn't accept American Express.

A note to yourself makes a good trigger if you can attach it to an event that's related to the behavior you want to catch. I recently got a fortune cookie reading "Resist impulses to change your plans." That's good advice for me, but I need it more when I'm about to accept a client's dinner invitation than when I'm in a Chinese restaurant. So I clipped the note to my appointment calendar, where it gives me a chance of staying out of serious trouble.

Tally Cards

Do you smoke too much or know somebody who does? As an amateur smoking consultant, I've managed to help dozens of people reduce their daily consumption just by having them write down the time when they take a cigarette. These people enjoyed smoking, and didn't want to give it up, but they *knew* they didn't enjoy every single cigarette and needed a trigger to remind them that they might be taking a cigarette unconsciously. I generally advise them to get a special cigarette case in which they can keep a tally card for writing the times. After keeping the tally for a week, they have not only reduced their smoking, but are enjoying it more when they do smoke. They've also transferred the trigger to the case itself and can dispense with keeping the tally.

We've used the tally card with similar success on many other habitual problems. To alter the habit of interrupting other people, I advise clients to keep a record of the time of each interruption and whom they are interrupting. To reduce the tendency to waste time on the telephone, I have them keep a list of whom they spoke to, what time they started, and what time they finished. In each of these cases, there's no requirement to *do* anything about the habit, except to gather information. Some people find that the habit isn't as bad as they feared: Their trouble wasn't the habit, but how they *felt* about it.

Physical Devices

I'm not the only overeater who needs a trigger. My friend Sid bought a bicycle chain and lock for his refrigerator door. The device wasn't to prevent him from getting at the ice cream, because all he had to do was go upstairs and fetch the key. But on the way up, he sometimes remembered his two heart attacks.

It's probably a good idea, however, to keep your triggers as private as possible. Other people may think themselves immune to The Main Maxim and make fun of you. Whenever Sid had visitors, he found the chain a bit embarrassing, and eventually he traded it in on an electronic device that says "Hello, fatso!" whenever he opens the refrigerator door. Unfortunately, the speaker wasn't nearly as effective as the lock and chain. Why not?

One reason was that the trigger came too late, because once he actually saw the food, Sid had a much more difficult time applying his knowledge. For a trigger to be effective, the timing must be perfect: Too late means you're already committed to the troublesome action, while too early means you may forget again betwixt the cup and the lip.

Other People

It's tempting to use other people as triggers, but it's a dangerous practice. I've sometimes asked people to remind me of something when all I really wanted was someone to blame when I didn't do what I was supposed to do. I finally learned to use my blaming as a trigger, to remind me that it was really my problem, not theirs. Consultants should keep this in mind when their clients start blaming them. You may want to be a highly paid scapegoat, but you should make a conscious choice.

Another problem with using other people is that people tend to trigger multiple associations. Sid told me that the male voice from his refrigerator reminded him of his father. When he was a fat teenager, his father tried to stop him from eating by ridicule and bullying. Like most teenagers, Sid learned to resist ridicule and bullying, so the trigger backfired. Instead of reminding him of his heart attacks, it reminded him that he had to resist being ridiculed or bullied. He ate an extra large snack to show that voice that nobody could push Sid around.

Signals

It's a good policy not to use people as triggers unless they volunteer for the job, and know exactly what they're getting into. To avoid abusing your volunteers, you must know about your own emotional reactions.

I've learned that I respond much better to hand signals than to words. As a consultant, I spend a great deal of time facilitating meetings. Hand signals are particularly effective at reminding me to shut up when I'm dominating the meeting by talking too fast, too long, and too loud. Verbal signals only exacerbate the situation, making me fear that someone else is trying to dominate the meeting by talking too fast, too long, and too loud.

I make pacts with my clients and students to give me hand signals when I forget myself, but the person I work with most is Dani, and she won't use them. Even though the signals stop me in my tracks with no feeling of anger, Dani finds them repugnant. To her, hand signals are a symbol of parental domination over children, the same meaning I attach to verbal interruptions. To me, hand signals are what referees use because verbal signals wouldn't be heard over the roar of the crowd; hand signals are just a normal part of the game. In the car, though, I accept verbal signals because I realize that hand signals would distract my attention from the road. Such is the logic of the illogical.

Mutual Trigger Pacts

When people are in the same business, trigger pacts may evolve without any explicit agreement. "You tell me when I'm doing it, and I'll tell you when you're doing it." But they must be mutual and symmetrical.

Computer programmers have had considerable experience with disaster, but they don't take kindly to being reminded by outsiders of the presence of icebergs. That's why they're custom-made candidates for The Titanic Effect. Yet I've earned some substantial consulting fees by triggering programmers out of the path of icebergs. I'm successful because programmers consider me to be a member of their guild. When I hear a programmer say, "What can possibly go wrong?" I can usually sound an effective iceberg warning merely by parroting the question.

I can also teach groups of programmers to ring the iceberg alarm for each other. I give them buttons reading "What can possibly go wrong?" I institute a circulating "Blunder of the Month" trophy. I teach them The Rule of Three. You might use these triggers to combat The Titanic Effect with any kind of client, but the triggers will work only if you're all in the same boat.

Paradoxically, mutual triggers won't work if you're all in *precisely* the same boat. If a food fit hit all its members at the same moment, Weight Watchers would turn into Grub Gobblers. All the members need the same trigger, but at different times. So, if your entire client organization is comfortably cruising on one *Titanic* voyage to nowhere, it's going to take someone from outside to shout "Iceberg!" And then, of course, your clients will say to the outsider, "What do *you* know about oceanliners?"

USING YOUR UNCONSCIOUS MIND

The Songmeister

Successful weight control programs are a living example of how triggers can be used to heed The White Bread Warning. In spite of the catchy name Weight Watchers, nobody ever lost an ounce through *watching* weight. Stepping on the scale and looking in the mirror consume less than one calorie each. What *is* effective is watching the *recipe* for gaining weight. When I was a little boy, my mother programmed me with the old family recipe for body fat. It worked beautifully for everyone in her family, and sure enough, it works for me.

My head is full of my mother's family recipes. For instance, there's an entire volume labeled "How to Create a Rebellious Teenage Son." This cookbook lay dormant in my brain until my own son Chris reached that notorious age. I received a note from his English teacher concerning his behavior. As I read the note, I found myself stewing with anger and broiling with plans for punishment. It was a nourishing recipe, and I savored my plans like a fine dinner.

I know I was savoring my plans because whenever I particularly enjoy a meal, I hum a tune. I'm usually too involved with real food to notice *what* tune I'm humming, but this time the food was only imaginary, so I noticed. I can't imagine where I learned this golden oldie, but it was "Just Before the Battle, Mother, I Am Thinking Most of You"—a perfect White Bread Warning. I was about to enter a battle with my son in which I would pass on the same recipe for rebellion my mother had so generously bestowed on me.

Since that time, I've become better acquainted with a peculiar region of my skull that hums songs to me when I need a trigger. Like "The Bells of St. Mary's" just a while ago. Or like yesterday, when Dani was planning a trip to New York. She hadn't been to her home town in a dozen years, and in her usual manner, she was making a list, this one of people she mustn't forget to call. Over supper, she asked me to check for omissions, but I couldn't come up with anyone. While I was washing the dishes, though, I caught myself humming the title song from Flotow's *Martha*. Years ago, I would have dismissed it as irrelevant humming, but I've learned to pay attention to whatever comes out of my head. As soon as I brought it to consciousness, I realized that Dani's list had omitted our good friend Martha.

Limits to the Unconscious

The unconscious is not an exact and analytical organ, so triggers from the unconscious aren't foolproof. In the midst of a five-inch downpour on the third day of hobbling along New Zealand's Milford Track with a painfully strained knee, I found myself humming "Yankee Doodle." Why? At first I thought it was merely homesickness. I know that I've received the correct message when the humming goes away, but the homesick explanation didn't do the job. After two maddening hours of "Yankee Doodle," I tried working through the lyrics. "Yankee Doodle went to town, riding on a pony. . . ." Eureka! My stupid songmeister was telling me that I could put an end to this miserable hike by getting a horse (terrific advice if I hadn't been in the midst of an inaccessible wilderness).

But I will say this for my songmeister: He's capable of learning, and of remembering things that I soon forget. When we lost power during last week's blizzard, I had to go out in freezing weather to service the generator. As I dressed for the cold, I found myself humming the tune to a panty hose commercial: "Nothing beats a great pair of L'Eggs." At Milford, my knee had seized up because I started hiking over a mountain pass in shorts without even warming up. I knew better, but forgot. This time, my songmeister reminded me: I didn't have any panty hose, but I did have long johns, I did warm up, and I didn't have a problem with my knee.

Watching the Inside of Your Head

Long before we were blessed with singing commercials, religious leaders understood techniques for planting their messages in memorable form. In the Bible, as in other great religious works, you find songs, poems, parables, paradoxes, checklists, analogies, and aphorisms. Some of them have worked for thousands of years for millions of people. They might be worth investigating if you want to build your own bell system.

Some of my students seem dubious about the possibility of developing their unconscious. One said wistfully, "You have an amazing unconscious, but I don't have one at all. And I don't think I ever met anyone before who had one." Certainly, it would be a waste of time to develop your unconscious if you don't have one, but the evidence indicates that most people do. But, by it's nature, it tends to be hidden from you unless you practice looking for it. Yours may not express itself to you in songs, like mine does, but perhaps it communicates through slips of the tongue, gestures, one-liners, puns, catchwords, flashes of mental pictures, body posture, inexplicable noticing of objects, mistaking one person for another, or a combination of several such phenomena.

Modern psychology explains this diversity by saying that the brain has multiple compartments. Different schools debate the exact contents and arrangement of the compartments, but most agree that we are influenced by all of them: left-brain, right-brain, conscious, preconscious, subconscious, or whatever. As scientists, psychologists are looking for a logical answer, but any brain that can remember "Just Before the Battle, Mother" can't be considered entirely logical. I'm a bit embarrassed to admit that my mind is so illogical, but it's the only mind I've got, and that's the way it is.

Besides, if the L'Eggs people spend their advertising millions on a combination of clever words and catchy tune, I can't be all that different from everyone else. So don't be afraid to cultivate your unconscious. If your friends laugh at you, let that trigger the thought that anyone who claims to have a completely logical mind has got to be crazy.

7

amplifying your impact

**Each person sees a part of the whole
and identifies the whole with that part.**

—Teaching the Blind

In one of my workshops, Karma told me about the day she was sitting in her cubicle reading a book called *The Supervisor's Survival Kit*. One of her supervisor's colleagues happened to come by and, when he noticed the title, said, "You shouldn't be reading that!"

"Why not?" she asked.

"Because you're not a supervisor."

Karma, who was never at a loss for the appropriate reply, smiled and said innocently, "Oh, do you want me to wait until it's too late, like they did with you?"

THE CONSULTANT'S SURVIVAL KIT

Although this book is ostensibly for consultants, I do hope that other people don't put off reading it until it's too late. I hope (and my publisher and my accountant also hope) that you read this book even if consulting is merely a slight possibility some time in your distant future. Even if it's no possibility at all, that is, if you're not a consultant yourself, you're likely to find yourself working with consultants, and that is a very good reason for reading this book.

Come to think of it, a supervisor's survival kit should be even more useful to a supervisee. Any good supervisor should be thrilled to see a worker learning about the problems of supervision. Supervisors aren't appreciated because most workers don't have a clue as to what supervisors really do. They see the rewards—the paycheck, the furniture, the power—but if the supervisor is doing a good job, most of the work itself is essentially invisible. The same is true of consultants. Many of my clients are impressed with my trips to exotic places, nights in posh hotels, meals in fancy restaurants, and fees that seem to dwarf their paychecks. They don't see the confusion of jet lag, the insomnia from strange beds, the indigestion from overeating, or the overhead and unpaid days that must be subtracted from my fees. Most of all, even when they work with me, they don't really see what it is I do.

KEEPING AHEAD OF YOUR CLIENTS

In the same workshop that Karma told her story, Larry told a story that explained why my clients don't see what I'm doing:

Zeke and Luke were hunting bear again. While they were taking a beer break, a bear came crashing out of the underbrush, heading straight for them. Zeke and Luke started running away, but the bear was rapidly closing the gap. "I don't think we can outrun the bear," Zeke panted.

"That's all right," Luke shouted over his shoulder as he pulled in front of Zeke. "I don't have to outrun the bear."

"Why not?"

"I just have to outrun *you*."

Like Luke, I just have to outrun my clients. Of course, it's not always easy to do that. They work at their jobs eight hours a day, and I come in a few days a year. When it concerns their day-to-day activities, there's no way I can even keep up with them. My success as a consultant depends, like Luke's, on being in the right situation, one in which the slightest lead is as good as a million miles.

To be successful, I must *amplify* my impact. I must work like a martial arts master, applying the slightest force and allowing the weight of my opponent to do the work. If I'm successful, my clients will experience change, but they probably won't notice that I've done anything at all.

JIGGLING STUCK SYSTEMS

The image of a consultant is quite passive. Consultants gather information and present it to the organization, which may or may not be affected. Although this sounds innocent enough, there's really no way to retain a consultant without causing some change to occur. This may sound threatening, but in many cases, a little disturbance may be good for an organization.

Getting Stuck

As electronic systems grow more complex, they begin to act more and more like living systems. For instance, many wild animals cannot breed or even be kept alive under laboratory conditions. The first radar systems were a bit like wild animals: They would work under combat conditions, but not in the sterile laboratory environment. Before World War II, no artificial system was sufficiently complex to display this dependence on a noisy environment, but we now understand that any large, complex system operating in an overly controlled and predictable environment can get stuck.

This sticking effect is another reason successful organizations fail. As organizations become better managed, their day-to-day operations can become so smooth that parts of the organization get "stuck" and cease productive functioning. This problem is particularly acute in those parts of the organization that are supposed to do new, creative work: research, development, training, and programming.

When a function begins to stick, some kind of jolt or jiggle from the outside may help. For radar, the problem was solved by attaching random motion generators to the racks, to break up the stable states in which the equipment tended to stick. These generators were called jigglers.

In organizations, a natural disaster such as a fire often has an invigorating effect. Strikes, when managers have to step into operational roles, sometimes give a similar shot in the arm. But it's not necessary for an organization to suffer the risk of arson or labor agitation in order to get unstuck. Instead, any outside, unpredictable, but nonthreatening agent can give the organization a jiggle.

The Jiggler Role

Some outside agents enter organizations as part of the natural order of business. New workers can serve this role. So can new managers. Sometimes, a consultant working on one problem can accidentally touch another area in which the organization is unknowingly stuck.

In recent years, the computer and the computer sales force have assumed the role of organization jiggler. When I worked for IBM, I myself often played this role, getting customers unstuck from problems that had nothing whatsoever to do with computers. At that time, however, I didn't realize that the jiggler was separate from the role of computer salesman or technician.

Later, during speaking engagements, I found that I spent one hour giving a speech and seven hours listening to people tell me their problems. I am not by nature a passive listener, so I often made jokes, uttered cries of disbelief, asked dumb questions, and sputtered grunts of non-comprehension. To my surprise, many people told me that my speech had solved their problem. I came to realize that it usually wasn't the speech, but these unstructured sessions before and after the formal part of the program, that solved the problems.

Over the years, I've discovered that what I do has no commonly accepted name. The best name would be jiggler, but who in his right mind would pay for the services of a jiggler? Sounds too much like juggler, or giggler, or even gigolo. So, after trying various alternatives, I still use the public name "consultant," although secretly I know I'm a jiggler. (My Tarot card is the Fool.)

As a jiggler, my job is to get something started, to cause some changes that will ultimately get the system unstuck. As a *systems* jiggler, I confine myself to working with *organizations* at various levels. Although I naturally work with both workers and management in my efforts to get things off dead center, I'm neither a psychiatrist nor personal confi-dante, but these can be jiggler roles as well.

Stuck by Overload

Perhaps the best way to understand what a jiggler does is to consider a few examples. A systems programmer complained that he was bothered by applications programmers all the time and could not do his assigned systems work. I sat alongside the systems programmer for a few hours, observing all his work habits and interactions with appli-cations programmers. I discovered that every problem involved reading dumps, the detailed printouts of the machine's full memory contents. The applications programmers didn't know how to read dumps effec-tively, so they turned to the systems programmer each time they had a problem.

I jiggled them at one level by observing that there are tools that format dumps so they can be read by the applications programmers. The systems programmer was delighted with this solution, but I knew that this problem might be merely a symptom of a larger form of organiza-tional stuckness. Therefore, I jiggled management with the following questions:

1.   Is it possible that nobody in the entire, rather large, organization knows of the existence of common tools like dump formatters?

2.   Isn't it surprising that so many applications programs are getting dumps in the first place?

3.   Is the training program so out of touch with the actual work done that programmers aren't taught to interpret dumps?

Working with questions such as these, I got the client to re-examine the entire department as a problem-solving organization. But even that wasn't enough. For the professional jiggler, there is always one more question:

4. Could the organization itself have generated the other questions? In other words, could it have jiggled itself?

With this question, I started the organization on the road to problem prevention, one level higher than problem-solving.

Stuck Communication

Here's another example. A project manager told me that she was worried about her team leaders. They didn't appear to appreciate that the project was in serious trouble. However, I could see signs of their fear when the subject of project schedule was broached. I asked the project manager to leave me alone with the five team leaders for half an hour and then proposed that each leader write an anonymous schedule estimate on a slip of paper.

The estimate gave the probability that the project would be done on schedule. The anonymity dealt with the fear. I gathered the papers and found that the highest of the five estimates was twenty percent! All five knew that the project was in serious trouble, but all were afraid to say anything in front of their manager.

Using a similar technique, I mapped out the probabilities of completion at various dates in the future. When the project manager returned, she gave her own figures for the same probabilities.

When the team leaders saw that their manager was equally pessimistic, communication began, and the team leaders admitted that they were afraid to speak their mind because they didn't know that the others felt the same way. Ultimately, project completion was rescheduled to a more realistic date, and steps were taken to assure that the new date would be met. Other measures were taken to ensure that future communication on the subject would remain open.

I was able to jiggle this stuck communication system because

1. I was a neutral person who would not betray any one individual.

2. I knew a technique whereby people could reliably but anonymously reveal their true feelings about the schedule.

3. I possessed general skills in facilitating accurate communication.

4. I understood how communication systems work, and how they could be established to avoid blockage in the future.

Opportunities to Jiggle

I'm seldom retained as a jiggler. Sometimes I'm engaged as a speaker, sometimes to perform a checkup, and other times as a consultant on a technical problem. But there are always opportunities to jiggle.

For one thing, people don't always see what their real problems are, so consultants are often employed to make the system get even more firmly stuck on the wrong problem. With software organizations, I'm often retained to improve quality by teaching the staff how to remove errors, rather than how to prevent them in the first place.

For another thing, when you have your eyes and ears open, you can't guarantee you'll observe only things that are relevant to the official problem. Nor can you guarantee that you'll only affect things that are relevant. I try to make my clients understand that their system is likely to be jiggled by my presence. If they find that prospect too frightening, then my consulting probably won't be effective, and so I usually turn down the job.

Giving a speech is a form of jiggling. An inspiring speech can do wonders for a stuck organization, but jiggling will fail if the arrangements are too formal. Most speeches are arranged under circumstances that will be "safe" to the organization—and that is as it should be. It's the function of management to keep things running smoothly; it's only when management is *too* successful that things running smoothly in the groove become stuck in a rut. Therefore, I try to arrange opportunities for jiggling to take place outside the speech itself.

Rather than being introduced as a speaker and consultant, I prefer to be introduced simply as "someone from outside with whom anyone can discuss matters of concern." When this concept is too difficult for management to swallow straight, I'll sometimes agree to come as a "speaker," provided there are many opportunities for unstructured consultation with members of the audience. I'll sometimes come as a "consultant," if I can avoid looking too much like a tool of management, which could destroy my usefulness as a jiggler.

The Law of the Jiggle

The Third-Time Charm described in Chapter 2 says that I may eventually become too closely associated with the organization's typical modes of thinking and problem-solving, and that when that happens I may lose my effectiveness as a jiggler. In such a case, I have to call on one of my own personal jigglers. If you're intent on jiggling others, it's important for two reasons that you experience being jiggled yourself: first, so you'll get unstuck; and second, so you'll know how it feels.

Because I've been jiggled many times myself, I have a sense of what kind of jiggling works best. Over the years, I've come to believe that the effectiveness of jiggling is governed by one simple law:

Less is more.

This is The Law of the Jiggle, sometimes called The First Law of Intervention.

In most cases, the only jiggling that's required is a tiny modification in the client's way of seeing the world. But how can we make such a change in a stuck system?

TEACHING THE BLIND

The Elephant

We're all familiar with the story of the blind people who tried to ascertain the nature of an elephant: Depending on what was first touched, each person got a different view. An elephant was like a tree, a snake, a rope, a house, a blanket, or a spear, with nobody able to grasp the entire picture. This fable reminds me of my clients' views of their own organizations. Each person sees a part of the whole and identifies the whole with that part. Often, my biggest job is getting the client to accept that other views are possible.

How do I go about doing that? Well, how would you teach blind people about elephants? You could, of course, *tell* them about elephants, which is what most consultants do. There's nothing wrong with telling, but it's surprisingly difficult for blind people and sighted people to communicate about their worlds. Their experiences are so different that simple words mean different things. What does a blind person understand from the simple phrase, "That's a gray area in the specifications"?

The same is true for consultants and clients. For instance, most of my clients simply don't know what it's like not to have a boss. If they do know, their picture is highly romanticized. Conversely, I once had a job, but that was so long ago I've lost touch with what it means to be an employee in a large organization.

Changing Perceptions

Before people can communicate effectively through words, they must have shared *experiences*. We might lead blind people around the elephant, allowing them to touch each part in turn, so that the entire group could experience the elephant. Companies that rotate their employees through different jobs and departments seem to develop people with richer perspectives. When consulting, I usually try to take a tour of the entire organization and, if possible, I get a person from one division to escort me to the next. Often, the escort remarks that the incidental trip to another division was the most significant part of my visit.

I can achieve a similar effect through mixed meetings, putting people from two or more groups together ostensibly as a way of "saving my time" for which they're paying by the hour, but actually as a way of getting them to experience more of the whole organization. Once I get group members in a room together, it's a little like the story of the Bible, which starts with Adam and Eve in a garden and ends in Revelation. There may be some bloody or tearful incidents along the way, but the revelations in the end are usually worth every bit of struggle.

Elephants and organizations are so big that it's hard to experience them whole. Sometimes, it helps to experience a scale model, such as a carved elephant or a simulated small organization, so I might give my blind friends a baby elephant or a newly formed organization to study. Babies, whether of the elephant or organizational variety, are both small and fast developing, so people can experience them *becoming* adults, which invariably leads to a better understanding of adults.

These ways all are excellent, but fall far short of the best way to teach blind people about elephants. The best way would be to actually cure their blindness. Unhappily, we can seldom cure the visually blind, but I can often cure my clients' perceptual hangups. Although I use a lot of show-and-tell and simulate direct experience in order to facilitate their understanding, my favorite method is to open clients' eyes to new ways of seeing things. Once their eyes are open, they'll continue to learn new things about elephants long after they've stopped paying my fees.

The Hippopotamus

By "new ways of seeing," of course I don't necessarily mean seeing with the eyes. There is an ancient story of the king who wanted a formula for turning lead into gold. He threatened his alchemist with death if he didn't produce such a formula, so the alchemist gave him a complex series of magical steps to perform. The king memorized the steps, then asked the alchemist if the formula was foolproof.

"Absolutely," he replied, "except . . . "
The alchemist hesitated, and the king demanded, "Except what?"
"Oh, it's really not significant. It couldn't possibly happen."
"What couldn't possibly happen?"
"Well, it's completely unlikely, but there's one thing that will ruin the formula. While you are carrying out the steps, *you must not think of a hippopotamus.*"

Changing Awareness

By this clever trick, the alchemist saved his life by putting the responsibility for failure on the king. I do the same thing when I tell a client:

"Don't be aware of your feet pressing on the floor!"

As you read that sentence, what happened? One moment you were seeing words on the page, shutting out most other aspects of your internal or external environment; at the next moment, your awareness changed, making it impossible for you not to be aware of your feet pressing on the floor. The more you *try* to obey the suggestion, the more you violate it.

I use this approach when trying to get clients to use nonverbal behavior more effectively. Most of us are more or less blind to nonverbal behavior. If I talk about it, many people simply don't know what I mean, much as a blind person would be mystified when told that an elephant is gray. After several direct experiences with their own nonverbal behavior, however, my clients no longer hold the vague concept of nonverbal behavior as a total abstraction.

Seeing Internal Behavior

We live in a culture dominated by talking, which is why we tend to be blind to a person's external behavior. *Internal* behavior, of course, is even less visible. Most of the time, we don't "see" our own internal behavior, and we almost never can see someone else's directly. With training, however, we can begin to see what might be going on inside someone else, and how that *might* be quite different from the external presentation.

Almost all of my consulting is conducted in some sort of meeting. If I can improve a client's meeting-effectiveness, my consulting task is simplified, and the client retains the benefits long after I've gone. The

Hidden Agenda is one of the techniques I use to train people to "see" inside others. I use the following technique.

Before a meeting begins, I give each participant a sheet of paper on which is written a secret personal assignment for that meeting. Here are some examples of such secret assignments:

- Try to see to it that every decision the meeting takes is written down and displayed so all can view it.

- Make sure that every person gets a chance to talk on every topic.

- Do not let any single person or clique dominate the meeting.

- Pretend that you have not prepared for this meeting, and try to conceal that fact from everyone else throughout the entire meeting.

- If at all possible, see that the meeting comes to decision X without letting yourself be identified with that decision.

The typical secret assignment describes something that people normally do in meetings, with some assignments having a positive effect, some negative, and some neutral. By playing the role explicitly, the actor learns to "see" behavior that was previously invisible, or to see alternative interpretations for behavior that was previously visible. This new vision inevitably affects a person's future understanding of meetings.

Two secret assignments I frequently use are these:

- Pretend you have another meeting to attend following this one. You very much want to attend that meeting, so do everything you can to make this meeting end as quickly as possible.

- Pretend you have another meeting to attend following this one. You very much want to miss that meeting, which you can do if this one runs overtime. Do everything you can to make this meeting last as long as possible.

By using both of these in the same meeting, I make it possible for everyone to see how the conflict works out. At the end of the meeting, I post a list of the secret assignments, and ask the observers to guess who had which. Without fail, the person assigned the "quick meeting" agenda is misidentified as the "prolonged meeting" person!

This happens because every attempt to rush the meeting—such as cutting speakers short, streamlining procedures, or pushing for quick votes—starts a conflict that prolongs the meeting. The person assigned to prolong the meeting finds that it's unnecessary to do *anything:* the job can be left to the "quick" person. Through this experience, participants learn the specific lesson that the best way to speed a meeting's progress is simply to keep quiet.

But more important, participants change their way of seeing what people do in meetings, and learn that the outward actions very often are precisely the opposite of the inward intentions. In doing so, they have made a small start toward seeing "inside" another person.

Seeing Feelings

Even though you've learned a little about seeing other people's thoughts, you still might be unaware of their feelings. Or even of your own feelings. For a consultant, seeing feelings is more important than seeing thoughts, but many people are as blind to feelings as they are to X-rays.

In order to get people more in touch with themselves, I used to ask them to write down their feelings in a personal journal. Sometimes, fully half of the people would stare blankly, writing nothing. They had no idea of what would be written under the heading of "feelings." Nowadays, we help clients get started with a list of words such as love, hate, disgust, affection, sadness, joy, pity, anger, sympathy, heat, cold, comfort, misery, nervousness, itchiness, or frustration. My friend Stan Gross starts them off with a simpler list of five feeling words, all of which rhyme: sad, bad, mad, glad, and sca'd (Southern for "scared").

The list of feeling words expands people's ability to see inside themselves, but for some this is still not enough. Although I've had dozens of participants tell me "I'm not feeling anything," it usually turns out that they are actually blind to their feelings.

With a little effort, I can usually find some feeling that they can safely identify. One participant said he had no feelings, but that sometimes he had "physical feelings." That phrase, for some reason, was safer or more meaningful, and provided a starting point for discovering feelings. It gave me a clue as to how to get started with other people who claimed not to have feelings.

I ask if they are hungry or thirsty, warm or cool. Can they feel a slight pain, itch, or discomfort anywhere? If they still say they feel nothing, I may take them through an inventory of their body, starting with the toes and working up. If they can feel their toes cramped in their shoe, it's a start and I can work from there, but if they still don't find anything by the time they reach the top of their head, I'm still not stumped. I can usually see by then that the person is genuinely confused, so I ask, "Are you confused by all this?" They usually reply with an eager yes, so I ask, "How do you *know* you're confused?" They then become aware that they know by some sort of direct experience, so I can point out to them that they now know what a feeling feels like—the feeling of confusion.

It's amazing how many times the ability to identify the first feeling draws an "Oh!" followed by an outpouring of other feelings. It's not that people hadn't understood the question, but that they were blind to feelings. Once they see the first one, their vision can develop. As a consultant, I can help them practice, but even without me, they're on their way to an understanding that can never be taken away. Yet without that first glimpse, the request to write about their feelings is literally as meaningless as asking a blind person to write about the color of an elephant's eyes.

THE POWERFUL CONSULTANT

If you keep amplifying your impact, you'll eventually become a more powerful consultant. Your consulting style will reflect an increasingly complex understanding of your task and will have the following characteristics:

- Your task is to influence people, but only at *their* request.

- You strive to make people less dependent on you, rather than more dependent.

- You try to obey The Law of the Jiggle: The less you actually intervene, the better you feel about your work.

- If your clients want help in solving problems, you are able to say no.

- If you say yes but fail, you can live with that. If you succeed, the least satisfying approach is when you solve the problem for them.

- More satisfying is to help them solve their problems in such a way that they will be more likely to solve the next problem without help.

- Most satisfying is to help them learn how to prevent problems in the first place.

- You can be satisfied with your accomplishments, even if clients don't give you credit.

- Your ideal form of influence is first to help people see their world more clearly, and then to let *them* decide what to do next.

- Your methods of working are always open for display and discussion with your clients.

- Your primary tool is merely being the person you are, so your most powerful method of helping other people is to help yourself.

Being a powerful consultant may sound desirable, but there are great dangers implicit in this approach to consulting. Since the most powerful method of helping other people is by helping yourself, model consultants tend to influence people by their very presence, even when their influence has not been requested. In a sense, once you become an effective consultant, you cannot go backward. You cannot really be *ineffective* in a situation, even if you want to be.

At times, I have found myself talking casually for an hour or two to my seatmate on an airplane. At the end of the flight, often my seatmate says, "After talking to you, I know that things are going to be different in my life." I've had strangers decide to visit a marriage counselor, change jobs, change majors in college, write a letter to a parent they haven't talked to for seven years, modify an international marketing strategy, refuse a tempting job offer, and many other smaller changes, all as a result of a few hours of talking.

This kind of influence used to frighten me. As I amplified my impact, I became a potentially dangerous person. Eventually, I understood that I was suffering from grandiosity. My role in these changes was almost trivial. These people were on the brink of making these changes, and if I hadn't sat next to them today, somebody else would have done it tomorrow. Or the next day. I was, at most, their trigger.

I know this model is correct because powerful consultants have triggered me in the same way. But even being a trigger carries a certain responsibility. We can't just waltz through the world triggering changes without caring about the consequences. Otherwise, we're no better than used car dealers who won't service what they sell.

At the very least, you need to understand about change—how it happens, how it doesn't happen, and how it can be effected more gracefully. These topics will be the focus of the next chapters.

8

gaining control of change

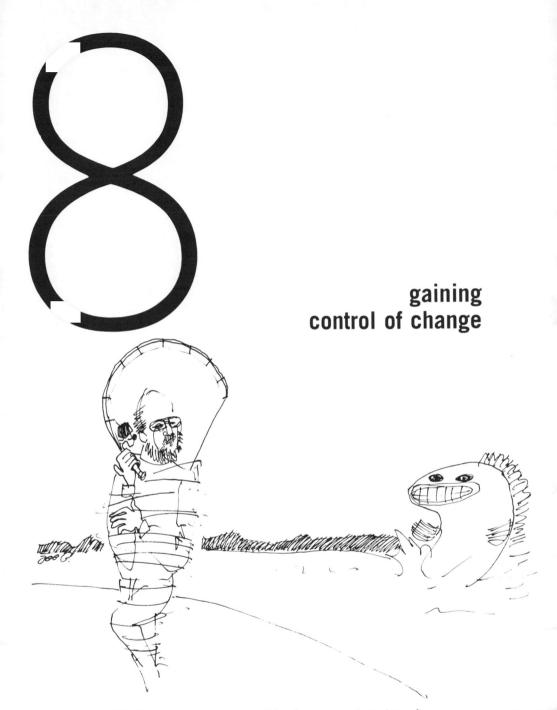

The best way to lose something is to struggle to keep it.
—Romer's Rule

I believe that consultants work by getting their clients to amplify small interventions. But how can the co-author of Weinbergs' Law of Twins believe that *any* change is possible, let alone change triggered by a single person?

This question arises from a common misunderstanding of Weinbergs' Law of Twins. Some people remember the law as saying

> **. . . no matter how hard people work at it, nothing of any significance happens.**

But the actual law has a preamble, and states

> **Most of the time, for most of the world, no matter how hard people work at it, nothing of any significance happens.**

which is entirely different.

Weinbergs' Law of Twins can be stated in other forms, to emphasize this other aspect. For instance, it can be turned upside down:

> **Some of the time, in some places, significant change happens— especially when people aren't working hard at it.**

Weinbergs' Law of Twins does not prohibit change. Any fool can see change everywhere. Every year, I notice that my pants are tighter, stairs are steeper, and print is smaller.

Because so many changes are for the worse, consultants are often called upon not to change things, but to keep them from changing. "Influence" does not always mean influence for change. In fact, there are probably more diet consultants, exercise consultants, and vision consultants than all other forms of consultants combined, all of whom spend most of their time trying to stem the tide of change. For them, at least, it would be a good idea to study the other side of Weinbergs' Law of Twins: how it is that change *ever* happens, and what can be done to prevent it.

123

PRESCOTT'S PICKLE PRINCIPLE

How can I explain how change is prevented? Let me tell the story of Prescott, who ran an old-fashioned country store:

Prescott's General Store was a model of authenticity, and so was Prescott. After disposing of a customer seeking frozen peas, Prescott settled into a wooden chair by the pot-bellied stove, perched his feet on the cracker barrel, and nodded his head in the direction of the front door. "*Frozen* peas! Land o' Goshen, what would I want with *frozen* peas! I've got seven varieties of dried peas, four sizes of canned peas, candied peas, smoked peas, and the world's finest pea soup put up in jars. Even if I was gettin' a freezer, which I ain't, I wouldn't stock it with *peas*."

"People nowadays seem to *like* frozen peas," I ventured.

"People nowadays don't know what's good and what ain't. Women who wear pants probably don't even know how to open a can without an electric thingamajig, let alone make a decent bowl of soup."

"Still, if you don't give people what they want, how are you going to stay in business?"

"I'm goin' to *resist*, that's what I'm goin' to do. There's a right way and a wrong way to run a store, and I don't care what anybody says; the old-fashioned way is the right way."

"Well, I have to admit that nobody else makes pickles like Prescott's Pickles."

"The recipe is a secret. Handed down by my pappy, and from *his* pappy."

"I don't want to steal your recipe, but I am trying to learn about how things are preserved. Is there anything you can tell me, in general terms, about the secret of making pickles?"

"Well, maybe," Prescott settled back in his chair. "My grandpappy used to tell a story about a stubborn cucumber. When he put it in the barrel, it looked around at the other cukes and was revolted by what had happened to them. 'Dadgum it,' he cursed. 'What's the matter with you guys? Have you no pride? No self-respecting cucumber would let himself get pickled without putting up a fight.'

"'But what can we do?' they'd ask. 'You can *resist*, that's what you can do. That's what I'm gonna do. No brine is going to get under *my* skin.'

"Then grandpappy would stop, and I would always ask him, 'What happened to the stubborn cucumber?'"

"And what did he say?" I asked.

"He said, 'Don't be foolish, boy. *If you stay in the brine long enough, you become a pickle.*'"

Perhaps *because* stability is so widespread, most change arises *from* stability in some way. What could be more stable than brine, which resembles the ocean itself? And what could be more perishable than cucumbers, which are vulnerable to heat, cold, bruising, drying, and a thousand other natural shocks.

Was Prescott's Pickle Principle The First Law of Change?

Cucumbers get more pickled than brine gets cucumbered.

I didn't want to think so. It went against all my romantic notions that the lone battler could win out against "the system."

For months, I wrestled with the problem, losing sleep and annoying my friends. I decided I must pay another visit to Prescott, to clarify his meaning. I passed the store three times before I recognized it. The old-fashioned decor had vanished, replaced by a chrome and plastic exterior. The hand-lettered "Prescott's General Store" sign was nowhere to be seen. Perhaps it was hidden behind the gigantic neon sign reading "Prescott's Pizza Palace."

Inside, I didn't recognize Prescott either. Gone were the bib overalls, the homespun shirt, the corncob pipe. Also gone was the country speech. "Well, give me five. It's Jer on the air. Do you dig the new place?"

"What happened to the Country Store?"

"No customers. Lost a thou a week, but now I clear three times that. Frozen pizza—there's the action."

"But what about the value of preserving the old-fashioned ways?"

"Oh, I'm still all for that old stuff. But if you're in business, you have to give the customers what they want. Besides, pizza has traditions, too. Here, try a slice of pea and pickle. It's my specialty."

"Thanks, Pres, but I've got to run. I've already had one pickle too many."

Beating the Brine

It was depressing to see what had happened to Prescott, mostly because I could imagine it happening to me. Another way of stating Prescott's Pickle Principle is

A small system that tries to change a big system through long and continued contact is more likely to be changed itself.

I'm a small person with big clients. And so are many other consultants, which explains why so many of them get pickled. Anthropologists go native. Psychiatrists go crazy. People who worked in the Bell System, once the world's largest company, used to say that they became "Bell-shaped," a condition that befell external consultants as well as internal staffers.

To avoid getting pickled, a consultant must not spend too much time with one client. If you can't avoid this, at least break up the time by working with other clients, even for free. As a staff person, you must not stay in one job too long. It's hard to be effective, though, if you're always switching jobs or clients. Change generally takes both time and continued contact, or at least one of the two. The challenge, then, is how to get the *client* in long, continued contact with some kind of brine, without the consultant even being present.

THE FORCES OF CHANGE

Roamer's Rule

As an external consultant, I fly around so much that I'm not so likely to be pickled, except by airline food. And fellow travelers. I recall one flight when my fellow traveler, in seat C, was a cowboy. In seat B was his guitar.

I thought that the guitar must really be valuable to rate a seat of its own. Then I realized why. "Hey, I know you. You're Roamer Lethelbeck, the folk singer. Hey, I love your voice."

Roamer blushed. "Well, thanks. But it's mostly done with electronics."

"I admire your modesty, but you had to have some talent to start with."

"It was more determination than talent."

"How so?"

"When my father died, he left me the family farm. He also left me a mortgage. I loved that farm. All I ever wanted was to spend the rest of my days raisin' pigs and popcorn. But farmin' didn't pay much, so I took to singin' in the local tavern to meet the mortgage payments."

"And then you were discovered?"

"No, I did have a loyal followin', but not enough to pay the farm's deficit. So I took to playin' in some of the larger towns, which paid better, but that kept me away from home more, so it was harder to run the farm well. Then, when the money finally started to amount to somethin', it all went into fixin' up the farm."

"I have only five acres, but I know how much you can spend."

"Well, we had 200 acres, which really wasn't enough. Then a neighbor died, and I had a chance to buy another 240 acres. In order to get the cash, I signed up for a tour of seven states—which was when my friends gave me the name Roamer. My real name is George."

"How long ago was that?"

"Let's see . . . almost 25 years. And I'm still roamin'."

"Do you still have the farm?"

"Sure. It's over a thousand acres now, with all the most modern equipment. We even have a solar-heated hog buildin'."

"I bet you really enjoy it when you're home."

"As a matter of fact, I don't."

"You don't?"

"No. You see, after travelin' for a while, I saved enough to retire to the farm. I tried it, but I'd grown accustomed to the life of a wanderin' minstrel. After three months, I signed up for another tour, and I've been goin' ever since. I'll probably die in an airport somewheres."

"That's the saddest thing I ever heard."

"Why do you say that? I *love* what I do. I'm no longer the same person I was when I inherited the farm."

It was then that I realized that Roamer had taken up traveling to preserve what he loved most: the farm. And then he had become pickled by traveling. That led me to postulate what I call Roamer's Rule:

Struggling to stay at home can make you a wanderer.

Homer's Rule

It turned out that Roamer's farm was in Nebraska, not far from my home. He had given his brother, Francis, a half interest in return for managing it all these years. As soon as the trip was over, I set out for Prairie Home to meet Francis.

"First thing you've got to do is stop calling me Francis," I was instructed as we shook hands over the gate. "All my friends call me Homer."

"Is that your middle name?"

"Nope. It's sort of after my brother, Roamer. He roams; I stay home."

"I guess you both inherited your father's love of the land."

"Not really. I was just a kid when Dad died, so I hardly knew him. I grew up being shuffled among my maiden aunts in Chicago, Denver, and New Orleans."

"After all that, you must have really wanted to settle down."

"Actually, I preferred the gypsy life. But I couldn't support myself. When Roamer needed a caretaker for the farm, we made a deal. When he came back, he would pay for my travels. Otherwise, I never would have agreed to do it."

"Where did you finally go? Did you make the Grand Tour?"

"No, my biggest tour is running over to the co-op in Waverly, then down to the bank at Eagle."

"You mean your own brother reneged on you, just so he could stay on tour?"

"No, no, no. He urged me to go. I had enough money to hire a really good manager and go anywhere. But somewhere along the line I'd gotten a bit fearful of the big wide world. Roamer even said he'd take me with him. But I don't know, after all these years, I just *like* staying home."

So, apparently, there was a Homer's Rule to go with Roamer's Rule:

Struggling to travel can make you a stay-at-home.

The Most Powerful Force for Change

Roamer had tried to remain a homebody, but in trying to keep what he valued most, he became a wanderer. Homer, on the other hand, had started as a gypsy, but in trying to stay a gypsy, had become a stay-at-home.

In my travels, I've run across dozens of similar examples. A loving husband tries to hold onto his wife, but drives her away with his jealous rages. A lonely mother tries to keep her favorite child at home, but becomes so possessive that the child runs away. A company tries to stick with its most successful product . . . and the rest is history.

It all makes sense. Change requires a powerful and unrelenting force, and what could be more powerful than the desire *not* to change? So, according to Prescott's Pickle Principle, it's the most likely cause of change.

Romer's Rule

The principle was clear enough:

The best way to lose something is to struggle to keep it.

I decided to call this Romer's Rule, combining the names Roamer and Homer. I gave both of them credit to remind myself that the same law that could make one brother stay home could make the other travel—a powerful law indeed. When I proudly announced Romer's Rule to Dani as we were preparing supper, she almost hit me with the flounder.

"You idiot," she laughed. "That rule was first enunciated a long time ago, by the great paleontologist Alfred Romer."

"How was I supposed to know?" I countered. "You're the anthropology professor."

Whenever I accuse Dani of being a professor, she punishes me by giving me a lecture. In this case, she spent the entire lecture waving the flounder at me, while she told me how Romer had used this rule to explain great changes in the fossil record.

"Suppose a situation in which the earth's waters became crowded," Dani explained, "perhaps because new types of fish were beating the older varieties in competition for food. Whatever the reason, there was limited food available, so any species that could obtain additional food would be favored.

"Suppose, too, that one species somehow adopted the practice of creeping out of the water for a few moments—holding its breath, so to speak—in order to nibble at plants growing at the water's edge. As seen by the other fish, this species was moving into the fourth dimension. From its own point of view, it was *temporarily* moving out of its favored environment in order that it might permanently survive in that environment.

"In other words, such fish came out of the water in order to stay in the water, just as Roamer went out on the road in order to stay at home. But once they made that first tiny step, the die was cast. After thousands or even millions of years, some of their descendants eventually reached the point where land, not water, was their primary environment. Some remained amphibious, but many couldn't go into the water at all."

CONTROLLING SMALL CHANGES

Romer's Rule says that the biggest and longest lasting changes usually originate in attempts to preserve the very thing that ultimately changes most. Consultants can use Romer's Rule to advantage when trying to change a large system, but what if the consultant has been retained to *preserve* that valued thing? Perhaps we'd better examine a classic case of gradual change more closely, to understand how the best intentions can get off track.

A Change That Makes No Difference

In the executive offices of Corporal MacAndrew's Arkansas Stewed Possum Company, Ltd., Harold Halstead is busy making decisions about proposed changes to their product, the Possum-Patty. Just now,

Harold is listening to another bright money-saving idea from another bright young culinary scientist, Jones. When Jones pauses with anticipation, Halstead knows it's time for him to respond: "How much will it save the corporation?" he dutifully asks.

Jones is ready with his figures. "The savings amount to a hundredth of a cent per Possum-Patty. We sell ten thousand million Possum-Patties per year, so the total savings is one million dollars per year!"

Jones has undoubtedly been working on this innovation for a year or more and now needs only a nod from Harold to crown his triumph. "That's certainly a substantial savings," Harold says, "but we must also consider the sacred trust bequeathed to us by our beloved founder, Corporal MacAndrew. You wouldn't want to change the secret formula upon which our entire success is based, would you?"

"Oh, no," Jones replies aghast, tapping his blue-bound report reassuringly. "Here are market analyses conducted over the past six months, which conclusively demonstrate that this money-saving modification makes *absolutely no difference* to customer perception and reception of the Possum-Patty. As far as anyone can tell, the new formula is *indistinguishable* from our current recipe. Corporal MacAndrew himself, may he rest in peace, would be unable to detect any difference."

"In that case," Harold says, smiling and rising at the same time, "you've done an excellent job. Leave your report with me, and if it substantiates your claims, we'll implement the new formula in our next revision."

When Jones has rounded the bend in the carpeted corridor, Halstead notices that he has fifteen extra minutes to add to his lunch hour. "Great," he thinks, grabbing his topcoat and heading for the executive exit. "I'll have time to dine at *Al Dente's*—on some *real* food. How could anybody with living taste buds ever put one of those oleaginous Possum-Patties in his mouth? How in the world can we ever have built such a mammoth enterprise on such a revolting product?" How indeed? Can it be that Harold Halstead and the entire Arkansas Stewed Possum Company, Ltd., have fallen for The Fast-Food Fallacy?

The Fast-Food Fallacy

In order for The Fast-Food Fallacy to be valid, we need two logical conditions: First, we must have *repetition* (providing some standard product or service a large number of times); and second, we must have *centralization* (accounting for the cost of providing the standard product or service).

Because of the repetition, a small savings on one item provides a large savings on all the items. But without centralization, this savings never accumulates enough in one place to make a difference. When the two factors coincide, the organization will inevitably yield to the temptation to make a change that will save substantial costs, but which will make no difference to the product.

But why should that matter, since tests have shown it makes no difference? It matters because it's a special case of what systems thinkers call Compositional Fallacy, the idea that no difference *plus* no difference equals no difference.

Suppose Jones's idea was to reduce the number of caraway seeds on the Possum-Patty from 100 to 99. Certainly nobody could notice this tiny difference in their salivating rush to devour some possum fat. And if Jones gets the idea to reduce the number of seeds from 99 to 98, it *still* won't matter. But in a large organization, this process doesn't happen only once. There are so many bright researchers, each wanting to remove one caraway seed, that we don't know where it all will stop. We don't know exactly *when* it will make a difference, but somewhere between one hundred caraway seeds and zero caraway seeds, we will violate Corporal MacAndrew's sacred trust.

Although it's easy enough to spot The Fast-Food Fallacy when it's phrased in terms of one hundred or zero caraway seeds, Harold Halstead at the central office never faces such a simple alternative. It's a few caraway seeds here, several grains of salt there, one milligram of possum gristle somewhere else, and a tenth of a second frying in the deep fat. In the end, though, The Fast-Food Fallacy is inescapable, because

No difference plus no difference plus no difference plus . . . eventually equals a clear difference.

The Strong and Unrelenting Force

Corporal MacAndrew, who was well-acquainted with both faces of a penny, would have put it more colorfully:

Mony a mickle maks a muckle.

The Corporal knew how to save money, and bequeathed to his corporation a preoccupation with savings. But he also had an "irrational" dedication to his original recipe, which protected his Possum-Patties from slow death by The Fast-Food Fallacy.

The Corporal's dedication to his recipe may have been irrational in origin, but its effect made perfect sense. Prescott's Pickle Principle works both ways. The unswerving dedication to the Corporal's formula acted like a brine in which the entire company was immersed, preserving the quality of its product in the face of a thousand attempts to make "insignificant" changes.

To achieve constancy amidst change, there has to be some strong and unrelenting force. In many successful companies, that force is provided by a strong, charismatic founder, like Corporal MacAndrew. As the company grows, one individual isn't strong enough, and one of two things happens: Either the company loses its force and changes the quality of its product, or the founder becomes larger than life, a religious symbol in the corporate culture. And a religious symbol, though irrational, can be a strong and unrelenting force.

Just because a force is strong and unrelenting, it doesn't have to be good. Romer's Rule tells us that many companies, many countries, many species, and many individuals have failed because they held on too tightly to the wrong things. The Corporal's successor, Harold Halstead, knows nothing about Romer's Rule, and demonstrates his own variation:

The biggest and longest lasting changes usually originate in attempts to preserve the very thing that ultimately changes most.

Halstead is a sophisticated, "rational" businessman. He knows that the Corporal's strong and unrelenting penny-saving is essential to the survival of the organization in "today's highly competitive business world." What he doesn't understand is that the business is being strangled by his own efforts to maintain profits by cutting expenses, one penny at a time, because he hasn't got the same unrelenting dedication to the original recipe.

Ford's Fundamental Feedback Formula

The strong and unrelenting force needed to prevent The Fast-Food Fallacy need not come from a strong, unrelenting individual. The Corporal MacAndrews of the world are exceptional, and most people, like Prescott, are too weak to resist the blandishments of cost-accounting logic. But there is an alternative that consultants can use to prevent their planned changes from turning rotten one tiny step at a time.

Although Harold may be puzzled about what's happening to the patties, he knows enough to dine at the neighborhood Italian restaurant. Sophisticated research may tell large organizations what's gone bad, but human beings still rely on their noses. That's why pollution is always a battle between corporate data-gatherers and ordinary citizens.

Many pollution situations meet the conditions of The Fast-Food Fallacy: large-scale repetition with a centralized cost-accounting function. Little by little, an industrial plant makes changes to improve processing efficiency, with none of those changes making "any noticeable difference" in effluents. In the end, the citizens living downstream from the plant can smell the difference, even though the engineers can prove there's no pollution.

According to legend, Henry Ford was once interviewed by Congress on the question of how to prevent river pollution caused by industrial plants. Ford pooh-poohed all the complex legislation that Congress was considering, proposing instead a single law that would "end river pollution once and for all." Congress didn't pass the law, but its two parts are worth remembering:

1. People can take any amount of water from any stream to use for any purpose desired.

2. People must return an equal amount of water *upstream* from the point from which they took it.

In other words, people can do what they want with water, as long as they themselves have to live with the consequences.

Why does this principle, which I call Ford's Fundamental Feedback Formula, prevent a gradual drift into pollution? There are two reasons:

1. It is *strong,* because without the water, there can be no industrial process.

2. It is *unrelenting,* because it is attached by law to an essential input to the process, and cannot be escaped even for an instant.

If Harold Halstead and his researchers were forced to eat Possum-Patties as a condition of employment, The Fast-Food Fallacy would never get off the ground.

Consultants seeking to preserve quality should first verify that the people responsible for quality are, in fact, downstream from that quality. Individuals who act obnoxiously are generally unaware of their behavior. Watching themselves on videotape often cures the problem in the twinkling of an eye. Insensitive bureaucrats are generally found in places where they never use the services they are supposed to provide, such as welfare and unemployment offices. Hard-hearted surgeons often soften the first time they undergo real surgery themselves.

So next time you're looking for a restaurant, find out if the owners eat there. If they do, the food might still not be to *your* taste, but if they don't, it won't be to *anyone's*.

THE WEINBERG TEST

Consultants are downstream from nobody. This gives them a difficult responsibility when instituting change for their clients. Clients realize that consultants are protected from the consequences of their own recommendations, which is one reason consultants are often the butt of nervous jokes. These jokes put consultants in the same category as professors. Professors claim that if a student passes the test, it was a brilliant course. If the student fails, however, they claim it was a stupid student. Under those conditions, it's never the fault of the professor, which makes it difficult to maintain an effective curriculum. Most universities solve this problem by prohibiting any measurement of their effectiveness.

Measuring Effectiveness

While attending a computer conference in Davos, I found myself listening to a panel of three professors who debated the subject of computer science education. After describing their three different approaches to curricula, the panelists solicited questions from the floor. Someone asked, "How do you measure the *effectiveness* of your curricula?"

Instead of a reply, there was much clearing of throats, hemming, mumbling, and hawing. The audience stirred in their seats and hooted remarks concerning the usefulness of colleges and the mental capacity of the professors. Finally, one of the panelists challenged the audience to propose their own measurements. When nobody else seemed willing to take the risk, I accepted the challenge.

"Imagine," I said, "that this conference is finished and you have taken the train to Zurich to fly home. You have boarded your flight and the doors have been locked when you hear the following announcement blare over the loudspeaker in an artificial voice:

Fellow passengers: Today, you are participating in a historic event, the first fully automated commercial flight. From this moment on, until you arrive at the gate at your destination, this plane is under the complete control of a microcomputer. There is no human pilot or co-pilot, but you need not be concerned for your safety. The program that controls the

plane was accepted as a thesis project for a doctorate in computer science at X University. Bon voyage!

"The true test of your curriculum," I continued, "is how you *feel* at that moment."

Apparently, the professors on the panel didn't think my test was helpful, but the audience broke into uncontrollable giggles. The moderator tried to restore order, but the audience seemed to have lost interest in what the panelists had to say, once the panel had labeled my test as ridiculous. I, myself, was feeling rather downhearted, for I had intended the test as a serious standard, the most serious standard I could imagine.

As the room cleared, I was approached by a short, white-haired man, sporting a goatee and wearing a three-piece gray suit. He addressed me in English with a German accent: "Professor Weinberg, I liked your test. Unlike the panel members, I believe it to be a serious test, and I wanted to tell you that it correctly measures my own curriculum."

I was delighted to have someone take me seriously, so I asked, "And how *would* you feel when you heard the announcement?"

His reply surprised me. "Oh, I wouldn't be worried at all. I would be completely confident of my safety."

"Really? Is your program that good?"

"Not at all," he answered, a twinkle in his eye. "But if one of *our* students wrote the system, it wouldn't even start the engines!"

Putting Your Money . . .

Over the years, whenever anyone asks me how to measure risk, I've recalled the goateed professor. Although there are many tests one might apply, The Weinberg Test seems to occupy a fundamental place in the hierarchy of all possible tests. In brief, The Weinberg Test asks,

Would you place your own life in the hands of this system?

Not all systems need such a severe test, so I have constructed weaker versions of The Weinberg Test, such as,

Would you risk your right arm?
Would you risk your left hand?
Would you risk your life's savings?
Would you risk a month's salary?
Would you risk $10 of your own money?

I've used the $10 test several hundred times with computer programmers who assert that their program is now bug-free. Ninety-five times out of a hundred, the programmer backs down and refuses to wager $10 that I can't find a bug in a reasonable amount of time. The other five times out of a hundred, I win $10.

It's not hard to be confident with *other* people's money. The essential element of The Weinberg Test is the requirement that the claimant risk something personal, rather than simply blabber some empty abstractions. As consultants, we're trying to apply Ford's Fundamental Feedback Formula to ourselves, at least conceptually. In street language, The Weinberg Test is called "putting your money where your mouth is."

When we consultants propose changes, the first thing we should do is decide what level of Weinberg Test we're designing for, then put our own feelings on the line. If human lives are at stake, then our own feeling of safety is the minimum goal. If money is at stake, then we have to personalize that money on a scale we'd feel if it were our own money.

In the engineering disciplines, it took many deaths to provide the motivation for improving the state of the art. Ships sank, bridges collapsed, buildings burnt, airplanes crashed, steam engines exploded. How many human lives will we have to sacrifice before consultants learn how to do it right the first time?

I hope we won't have to sacrifice any. But what about other sacrifices—of time, of money, of human comfort? When life or death is not directly involved, we haven't done so well at personalizing the outcome. Perhaps The Weinberg Test could save more than lives. Perhaps it could save our jobs, our reputations, and even our self-respect.

9

how to make changes safely

It may look like a crisis, but it's only the end of an illusion.
—Rhonda's First Revelation

Winston Churchill once remarked that he was happy he wasn't a radical in his youth, so he wouldn't turn out to be a reactionary in his old age. As people grow older, they learn about how change works, which could easily cause them to be discouraged.

What kept me from turning reactionary was the comfortable income I was earning as a consultant, playing the midwife to change. Prosperous midwives don't go out of business just because many deliveries are fraught with complications. In fact, it's *because* of complications that midwives become prosperous. So instead of being discouraged, I turned my inquiries to ways of lowering the risks of change, just as a midwife learns to lower the risks of childbirth.

PANDORA'S POX

Pill-taking is a good example of the risks we face when tampering with change. Some time ago, I was having trouble with arthritis, so my doctor gave me a prescription for some pills. They relieved the pain, but upset my stomach. The second prescription didn't upset my stomach, but didn't relieve the pain either. Figuring that the doctor, like any consultant, would do best on the third try, I went back for yet another prescription. I was right. My stomach was as quiet as a snowdrift, and even on the first really cold morning of winter, my joints let me sleep soundly.

I wanted to stay under the electric blanket and enjoy the warm feeling a little longer, but a cabinet door slammed in the kitchen. As I rubbed my eyes awake, I realized that my whole body was lacquered with sweat and that I itched furiously.

My Pox

Dani was looming over me. "What's wrong?" I asked, temporarily putting aside my own discomfort.

"In the first place, my new digital alarm didn't work this morning, so I'm an hour behind schedule."

"That's too bad," I sympathized, "but as soon as you've had a cup of coffee, the world will look manageable."

"That's the second place. The new combination coffee maker/ grinder just ground itself to pieces. The blade tangled with the filter mesh and there are shreds of metal in my coffee."

"Is that all?"

"That was *enough,* until you started screaming. Can't you take care of your own problems, at your age?"

"I don't know. Turn on the light and look at my skin."

"Omygawd! Your face!"

"It's not just my face. It's all over . . . except maybe the soles of my feet. I can't *see* the soles of my feet. It must be my new arthritis pills. . . ."

"The ones that aren't supposed to upset your stomach?"

"They *don't* upset my stomach."

"They will if you look at your face."

"Would you call the doctor? It might be dangerous. I'll go look at the coffee maker."

The coffee maker was a total loss. While I was searching for instant coffee, Dani came down with the news from the doctor. "She says to get right over to the emergency room." As an afterthought, she added hopefully, "Maybe *they'll* have coffee."

I felt too feverish to drive, so while I dressed, Dani went out to start her car. While I was trying to cram my swollen foot into a shoe, she returned with an announcement. "My battery's dead. I think it might have something to do with the new battery charger I got for my tape recorder!"

The itch was getting worse. I was beginning to lose my patience. "Don't worry about that. We'll take my car."

"We can't. It won't start either."

"It *has* to start. It's brand-new."

"It may be brand-new, but I think the diesel fuel is frozen. It's more than a little cold outside."

With the help of the auto club, we got to the emergency room two hours later. I was fortunate it wasn't a life-threatening emergency, because there was another two-hour wait before I saw the doctor.

When the doctor finally arrived, she was most apologetic. The problem seemed to be that the hospital had just instituted a new computer-controlled procedure for scheduling medical personnel in the emergency room. "There are still a few bugs, evidently. I hope you weren't too miserable."

The New Law

Actually, I'd put the misery to good use. With Dani off to work, I scratched myself and reflected upon the accumulation of torments.

"There's got to be a reason," I told myself as I peeled away another layer of epidermis. "Too many things have gone bad at once to be a coincidence. What do all these disasters have in common?"

Taking up a pen so I'd stop scratching, I soon produced the following list:

New digital alarm goes into hibernation.
New coffee maker shreds itself into shards of metal.
New medicine causes third-degree itch and fever.
New battery charger drains car battery.
New diesel car fails to start because fuel has turned to Jello.

I couldn't see the connection right away, but the moment the doctor apologized for the hospital's *new* computer, I had it. If I hadn't been so crazed with fever, I would have seen it sooner:

Nothing new ever works.

After a few days, the itch had vanished, but the principle remained. Everywhere I looked, every story I heard, the principle was confirmed. The new puppy ate the bath mat. The bank's new posting system swiped $6,000 from my checking account. The new fighter plane flipped upside down the first time it crossed the equator. The new defensive formation gave up the winning touchdown with 47 seconds left to play.

I thought of naming this stupendous principle The New Law, but when I told Dani about my discovery, she merely yawned and changed the subject. When I persisted, she set me straight. "There's no sense writing about *that*. *Everyone* knows that new things never work."

"Then why is 'everyone' obsessed with changing everything for something new?"

"If you answer *that*, you'll have something worth writing about."

Pandora, Archetype of Change

I dragged out my history books. No matter how far back I went, people always seemed to know that nothing new ever works. Yet people always craved something new. Then I reached the very beginning—the Greek myths—and found the key.

We all know that Prometheus (whose name in Greek means "the one who foresees") stole fire from the gods. Zeus was outraged and conjured up a fresh torment for mankind—a living doll of clay and water, a virgin of irresistible beauty. Pandora, the living doll, was sent as a gift to Prometheus' brother, Epimetheus ("the one who reflects after the event").

Although Prometheus warned him, Epimetheus couldn't resist this new toy, and took Pandora into the ranks of humankind. Pandora came equipped with a great vase (not a box, as current versions assert) filled with all the afflictions that the gods could imagine. When she raised the lid, loosing these afflictions upon us, she became the archetype of all change.

The Worst Affliction

That much of the story we all know. But there's one more piece, for the single greatest affliction remained trapped in the vase. Unfortunately, it was released on a second peek, for without that affliction, we might have learned Pandora's lesson.

The trapped affliction was *hope*. As long as hope remains, people make the same mistake over and over and over and over.

This is the truly great discovery:

Nothing new ever works, but there's always hope that this time will be different.

Surely this law deserves a trigger name, and what could be better than Pandora's *Pox?* It wasn't the grisly contents of Pandora's Box that gave us the incurable itch for every new whatsis. It was our own hope.

LIVING WITH FAILURE

Pandora's Pox is a social disease, spread by marketeers. Like most social diseases, it's endemic. And don't hope for a technological breakthrough to eradicate Pandora's Pox. You *know* no breakthrough ever works, but your clients seem to be suckers for every new fad. Rather than fight change, a more sensible approach is to learn to live with it. Or to make a living from it.

The Dealer's Choice

If those marketeers keep coming around, your clients are sure to succumb to some of their blandishments, so why not go with the flow. As my friend Henry was fond of saying,

Trust everyone, but cut the cards.

Or, in the present instance,

Let them try whatever they like, but teach them how to protect themselves.

I call this principle The Dealer's Choice, because as a consultant, you're dealing the cards. Your clients have to be in the game, but you can stack the deck for them by helping them establish a *series* of defenses when they are trying some new deal.

Accept Failure

The first line of defense is accepting that the new system *will* fail, possibly in several ways. When I find myself thinking, "I must have this change because I *can't* afford failures," then I'm in big trouble. If I can't afford *some* failures, a new system won't help. And neither will an old one.

Once I accept that failure is inevitable, my next defense is to ask myself a different question: "Why do I have the impression that I can't afford even some failures?" The new alarm clock is a good example. Have you ever lost sleep wondering whether the alarm would wake you for important business?

Trade Improvement for Perfection

What's the one thing that's worse than not waking up? Not going to sleep. Which suggests my next defensive question: "If the new system can't be perfect, how can I use it so it will be *better* than the one I have now?" Improvement is easier than perfection, and as the Chinese say, the best is the enemy of the good.

For instance, I can use my new alarm to supplement the old one. With two alarms, my chances of waking on time have to be better—or at least no worse.

Apply The Rule of Three

The next line of defense is to spend thirty seconds considering how this better way of using the system might fail. Applying The Rule of Three, I may not catch everything, but I always catch a few of the big ones that would otherwise get away.

How many ways can you think of that a new alarm clock could fail? Here's my thirty-second list:

1.   power failure

2.   batteries put in wrong

3.   setting the alarm wrong, due to unfamiliarity

4.   plug pulled out of the wall because the cord looks like that of another appliance

5.   alarm goes off, but it's not recognized as an alarm

6.   reading the time wrong and going back to sleep

7.   Dani turns it off because the sound is annoying

I wouldn't have considered any of these possibilities if I'd been dazzled by the vain hope that the new alarm wouldn't fail. Yet they're all easy to protect against, if only by using a backup system.

Invent a Backup

The next line of defense is to *invent a backup*. The alarm backup is simple: Provide another alarm. But that's not the only possible backup. Some of the failures can actually be turned into backup methods, given a little twist.

The unfamiliarity of the new alarm is a good example. I can tell Dani that I'm using a new alarm and want help responding to the new sound. This not only protects me against 5, 6, and 7, but also against 2, 3, and 4. If Dani wakes up and finds me still making ZZZZ's, she's authorized to wake me. Human backup systems are nicely adaptable.

Dani's new coffee maker could have been backed up by a jar of instant coffee. The coffee wouldn't be as good as freshly ground and freshly brewed, but it ought to be tastier than a cup of hot water.

PREVENTIVE MEDICINE

Although backup systems are the last line of defense, they some-times fail, too. When Dani's car battery failed, my diesel fuel froze on the same day. Both involved relatively new systems. Even though I could tolerate one new system failing, I wasn't able to defend myself against two simultaneous failures.

The Edsel Edict

And speaking of failed cars, consider the Edsel, the Ford Motor Company's great flop of the Fifties. I was a consultant to Ford on the Edsel, which makes me something of an authority on Pandora's Pox. Even so, I've kept my mouth shut for twenty-five years because I didn't truly understand what happened to the Edsel. Then, recently, Ford began a Better Ideas campaign, and I reconsidered my position.

In my memory, the Edsel project was a great triumph. We installed some terrific new computer systems that ultimately were adopted by the entire auto industry. Even if the Edsel didn't sell, *our* ideas were vindicated. After meeting many former Edsel people over the years, I've discovered that they *all* feel the same way I do. They got involved in the Edsel because they had a vision of something new—another "better idea" from Ford.

The Edsel, it turns out, was Ford's way of taking care of *all* their better ideas in the 1950's. Consultants and other fanatics with new ideas are dangerous to the established order, so why not put them all in one place, out of harm's way. That approach guarantees that even if each of the individual ideas is terrific, the result will be a debacle. As a consultant, I've seen this approach to avoiding change many times since my Edsel days, but never with such refinement.

No backup system in the world, no series of defenses, will protect you from failure in the type of situation that produced the Edsel. Only preventive medicine might have helped, so let's honor that noble antique by naming one preventive bit of advice The Edsel Edict:

If you must have something new, take one, not two.

In other words, if you must sleep with a new partner, use your old alarm clock. Or, if you must get a new alarm clock, hang onto your old spouse.

Choosing Your Time and Place

Another approach to protection against Pandora's Pox is to choose the time and place to put the change into effect. If you're trying your new alarm clock, wait for the weekend, or the day you've nothing on at the office until noon. Better yet, wait for the day you're visiting your in-laws. If you buy a new car—or a used car, for that matter—don't drive it off the lot and onto a 14,000-mile vacation. Take a short trip, even a few short trips, to shake it down. Stay close to the dealer so you can afford the towing bill.

But sometimes you don't have a choice. Dani and I once took seven of her students on an anthropological field trip through Europe, using a nine-passenger Volkswagen bus that we took delivery of in Luxembourg. Since we couldn't very well get the bus delivered to us a few months in advance in the United States, we were stuck with the uncertainties of a new vehicle from Day One. In a new country, with a newly assembled group of nine people, we would have served ourselves with a foolproof recipe for disaster had we not taken out some insurance.

The Volkswagen Verity

We saved our skins and our tempers by applying The Edsel Edict, systematically reducing the newness one feature at a time. We began with the new people. Starting three months before our departure, the entire group met one evening a week, ostensibly to discuss field work. In the process, however, we got to know each other better. When we were ultimately packed like nine sardines in a tin, life was a bit more tolerable. Not civilized, mind you, but tolerable.

A month before we left, we borrowed a similar van and practiced short trips. We also did a dry run on packing our luggage. Stripping down to essentials was universally painful, but it would have been excruciating in Luxembourg.

By adopting this strategy, we managed to confine the newness to the minimum essential areas: mostly the VW bus itself. But come to think of it, the VW bus was a tried-and-true product. Snorri, our bus, may have been new, but she followed a time-tested design. Unlike an Edsel.

Edsel tried too many new features at once. Volkswagen, on the other hand, is a company famous for its deliberate policy of introducing one small change at a time, and testing that change any which way possible. To The Edsel Edict, we can add The Volkswagen Verity:

If you can't refuse it, defuse it.

There are many strategies for defusing newness, such as,

- making practice runs in a similar situation
- breaking the newness into parts, to be adopted singly
- letting others share the breaking-in

You can apply The Volkswagen Verity to buying a car or building a vast computer network. Before you buy that Warthog 440Z, rent one on your next trip. If you've been driving an automatic, but are switching to the Warthog four-on-the-floor, rent an automatic first to give yourself a chance to get used to the *other* new features. And above all, don't be the first on your block.

If you can hold your horses for a few months, other Warthog owners will ventilate their gripes, most of which you can stop, side-step, or soften. Hopefully, the Warthog people will also come to grips with the gripes. Or at least the service people will have lots of practice. In short, ignore the sales pitch: Buy your Warthog near the end of the model year.

The Time Bomb

These strategies do work. You really *can* beat Pandora's Pox, some of the time and as long as you don't start to believe you can beat it all the time. My clients have successfully used these strategies for hiring new employees: Hire them one at a time, allow a generous breaking-in period of lowered productivity, give them meaningful but not critical work to do, and provide backups for their inevitable failures. They've also used the strategies for installing computers: Add one unit at a time, provide a generous breaking-in period of lowered productivity, use them for meaningful but not critical work, and provide backups for the inevitable failures.

When I recommend these strategies, the most frequent objection is that they "waste time." People always seem to be in a hurry to get new things working. Now that's only reasonable, for if they weren't impor-tant, we wouldn't be bothering with them in the first place. But time pressure blows holes in new things the way steam pressure blows holes in new boilers. That's why I have a trigger that pops whenever I hear "We're wasting time." I call it The Time Bomb, and it says

Time wounds all heels.

Or, put another way,

The surest way to waste time is to throw caution to the winds.

I was called in by a new client to help prevent the repetition of a million-dollar loss caused by one person who crashed their new infor-mation system—twice—on the first day they opened a terminal to the public. All he did was flip the terminal power switch on and off a few hundred times in a row. (He did this so he could watch the curious light pattern on the screen.)

The client had prepared for opening the system to the public by going through *some* of the defenses in my procedure. Managers brainstormed many ways the terminal could cause failure, and the DP people designed better systems to prevent those failures. But in the end, they were in a hurry, and they had too much confidence, or hope, that the system wouldn't fail. The effect was predictably *Titanic*-like.

Because of their confidence, they wouldn't accept that failure was inevitable, so they neglected to provide a backup. All they would have needed was an informed person standing by the terminal for the first few days, but they wanted to save their valuable time, so the nearest knowledgeable person was forty-five minutes away. And, they were in such a hurry to get the system going again that they couldn't wait until they got somebody out to the terminal. By the time someone reached the terminal, the system had been crashed again—by the same person using the same method.

Heeding the wisdom of The Time Bomb rule could have saved my client a half a million dollars when it set up the public terminal. Following the rule would have saved the client another half a million after the system crashed the first time. The client did prevent the loss of a third half-million, but it was an expensive way to build a bell system.

RHONDA'S REVELATIONS

I was disturbed by my inability to prevent my client's first two system crashes. I knew better, but it seemed to take a crisis to motivate that particular client to change. Much of the change I see is motivated by crises. Motivation by crisis isn't the most clever way to do things, but as a consultant, I have had to learn how to deal with it. I learned much of what I know about crises from my friend Rhonda.

Rhonda is a research biologist. I've always admired her cool manner of handling the toughest situation. Recently, she married a man with two small children (enough to turn hairs gray on any normal person), but Rhonda seemed to take it all in stride.

The only apparent change to her efficient office was a framed color photo of hubbie and the kids. Adopting her efficient manner, I got right to the point. "I came to ask you about change, and to learn whether it's possible for people to change without going through a crisis."

"Okay, let me tell you a story."

Crisis and Illusion

"When I decided to marry Peter," Rhonda began, "all my colleagues asked me whether my new instant family would affect my work.

What made them think that a scientist who manages $3,000,000 in grants, 14 young laboratory assistants, and 150 aging beagles couldn't manage a household, two kids, and a husband?"

"Maybe they were just making conversation."

"Well, I took it as an insult. I wasn't about to be mistaken for some fluff of a housewife, some pickle in one of Prescott's barrels. The day we got back from Fiji, I had the entire daily routine orchestrated like Beethoven's *Ninth Symphony*. It was a work of art."

"I can believe it."

"The boys were at the breakfast table, like the violin section, spooning in Quaker Oats. And Peter was playing first cello on his slice of ham with his steak knife. Out in the driveway, the station wagon was humming like the double bass, full of gas and warming up for a comfortable ride to Brian's day-care center and Ethan's Montessori school."

"What instrument were *you* playing?"

"I was the conductor, of course, stirring my coffee with my baton. I remember thinking that it was just like running the lab. All it took was organization. Then I happened to glance out the window—just in time to watch Mendel, our cat, being hit by a car!"

"Killed?"

"Squashed like a raisin in a wine press. But do you know what the first thought was that came into my head?"

"No, what?"

"I thought: *You can't be killed now. There's no time in the morning schedule for grief.*"

"Amazing! So what did you do about it?"

"I flew to pieces, that's what I did."

"I don't believe it, Rhonda. You're not the crisis type."

"You don't think so? That's because you still don't understand about crises. That morning was not a crisis."

"It sure sounds like a crisis."

"For the first five minutes, I thought it was a crisis, too. Then I had a revelation: It wasn't a crisis at all, it was the end of an illusion."

So that was Rhonda's First Revelation about change through crisis:

It may look like a crisis, but it's only the end of an illusion.

The Struggle to Preserve

I could understand Rhonda's revelation, but it was a little hard to believe that all crises were simply the end of some illusion.

Rhonda understood my difficulty. "Once in a very great while," she said, "there's a real crisis . . ."

". . . like when your cat is squashed like a grape?"

"No, that was just an illusion, too."

"It seems to me that a flattened cat is no illusion."

"But it was. In the midst of all the yelling, Mendel came up from the cellar, crying for his morning milk."

"He survived the accident?"

"He wasn't even *in* the accident. My illusions were so ripe for popping that when I looked out the window, I imagined the worst. Actually, the car ran over a soccer ball."

"So the illusion ends—and you make it worse by actively trying to hold onto it?"

"Exactly," Rhonda said, smiling. "Take your mid-life crisis. Do you remember? You stopped believing that you were going to live forever, in perfect health, and never get fat. Right?"

I winced. "The hardest part is when teenage girls open doors for me."

"For me it's dropping my image of absolute competence."

"But you *are* competent. You're the most competent person I know."

"But not *absolutely* competent. You're just sharing the illusion I tried so hard to make into a reality."

"Well," I said, "you did a good job."

"Of course, I did a good job; I worked hard enough at it. And why did I do it? Because

"When change is inevitable, we struggle most to keep what we value most."

Illusions Only Make It Worse

Rhonda's Second Revelation has proved even more useful than the first. Whenever my clients struggle in the face of change, I can use that struggle to discover what they value most. Sometimes, I can even catch myself struggling, and learn something about my own values. I was certainly struggling against Rhonda's revelations, a fact that she didn't fail to point out.

"What is it you don't want to face about these revelations, Jerry?"

"Admitting that I make my clients believe they need me in order to change. And that's because I fear that they *don't* actually need me, and that I will lose them."

"Precisely."

"This is awfully hard to take, Rhonda. I don't like to believe that about myself."

"Of course not, but you shouldn't be ashamed. It's a law of nature. My beagles protect their puppies; you, your clients; me, my competence."

"Well, if beagles do it, why is it so bad to protect what you value?"

"Not for any moral reason, but because of the trouble it creates. Beagles have the sense to stop protecting once their puppies are grown up. But people can create illusions, which they build to replace the lost reality. Most real change is a slow process. Like aging. But when we build illusions to hide the change, we soon find ourselves spending all our energy maintaining the illusions. That keeps us from dealing with change while it's still small. It's the crash of illusions that makes us believe change happens as crises."

"And it's the energy we put into preservation that makes the crisis worse?"

"Exactly. You might say that's my final revelation."

When you create an illusion, to prevent or soften change, the change becomes more likely—and harder to take.

Rhonda's Third Revelation applies to all possible approaches a consultant might use to help a client deal with change. Whatever approach you use, do it in an open, clear manner. That's the greatest service you can offer a client, because when difficult changes begin, truth is always a scarce commodity.

You should also encourage your client to face the truth at the earliest possible moment. If you really care about "protecting" people, don't ever "protect" them from the truth. The truth may hurt, but illusions hurt worse.

10

what to do when they resist

You can make buffalo go anywhere
just so long as they want to go there.

—The Buffalo Bridle

Even after providing backups for all the risks of large changes and all the pitfalls of small ones, consultants are confronted with people who don't seem to want to change at all, people who sometimes have excellent reasons. What people do to prevent directed change—their resistance—ranges from outright sabotage to more sophisticated forms, such as the "help me/don't help me" game. The one form of resistance I rarely see is a simple statement, "No, thank you. I don't want to change."

APPRECIATING RESISTANCE

Every consultant complains about resistance, but if you think resistance is bad, consider the alternative: It's frightening to encounter a client who doesn't resist your ideas, because that places the full responsibility on you to be correct at all times. Since nobody's perfect, we need resistance to test our ideas. So, the first step in dealing with resistance is to *appreciate it* for the way in which it makes the consultant's job easier.

Fortunately for consultants, resistance is universal. All successful consultants have tools for handling resistance, whether they know it or not. The approach I use is an extension of the work of Peter Block, who wrote *Flawless Consulting: A Guide to Getting Your Expertise Used*, an essential book for all consultants. Look for more detail there, but in this chapter I review Block's major steps.

GETTING THE RESISTANCE OUT IN THE OPEN

Resistance is like fungus. It doesn't thrive in daylight. Therefore, once you suspect that there is resistance, your next step is to get it out in the open, rather than let it fester in the dark.

Your Reaction

Whenever I feel resistance to my ideas, my first instinct is to resist the resistance. If I'm repeating myself, or exhibiting any peculiar behavior, my unconscious has already recognized the resistance and is trying to combat it. My conscious mind is slower to realize what's going on, but when it finally gets into the act, my most reliable resistance detector is direct observation of my own behavior.

You should get acquainted with your own behavior pattern. At the slightest hint that something may be out of kilter, follow Brown's Brilliant Bequest and start listening to your music. Notice nonverbal behavior, which will either be defensive or aggressive, depending on how you perceive the resistance. Here are a few of the actions you may catch yourself doing:

Defensive	*Aggressive*
—moving away	—pointing finger
—looking away	—staring downward
—shaking head no	—shaking head yes
—crossing arms, legs	—shaking fist
—excessive smiling	—excessive frowning
—yawning	—drumming

Having noticed one of these actions, I can usually trace it inward and find that I'm feeling bored, annoyed, impatient, or angry. Sometimes, I detect the feeling directly, without noticing any unusual nonverbal behavior. At other times, my clue comes from the way I'm speaking—not the content, but the form. I often catch myself saying "I" or "you" instead of "we," or speaking in a tone of voice that I can best describe as "parental."

Their Action

I can also detect resistance through the nonverbal behavior of the other people, although I find this technique slower and less reliable because I don't have access to other people's inner feelings.

As a last resort, I listen to their words, but this is the least reliable method of all. Many people are skilled at concealing their resistance in words, though sometimes I can trigger on such key phrases as

"I need more detail."
"You need more detail."

"It's too soon."
"It's too late."

"The real world is different."
"I have a theory about it."

"That's never been tried."
"That's old stuff."

"I don't have a problem."
"I have too many problems."

I've listed these in contradictory pairs, not just to make them easier to remember, but because they often occur in such pairs. It's as if the resisting person were saying, "I'll say whatever is necessary to counter these changes."

Paradoxes are also common, so even if I don't hone in on any specific words that would indicate resistance, I still catch many contradictions. Two of the most common verbal clues to resistance don't require your listening to the words at all. Sometimes, there will be a long *silence* at a point that would naturally call for a response. Sometimes, just the opposite will occur: a long, meaningless babble.

But perhaps the most common manifestation of resistance is when the client turns on me and says, in effect, "*I* don't have a problem, *you* have a problem." It's an obvious contradiction, because the client is paying me to work on a problem, not vice versa. It's common because it's effective, and it's effective because sometimes it's true. Sometimes, the consultant does have the problem.

I certainly have problems, and sometimes I project these problems onto my clients. That's why the next step in the process is so crucial. Whatever else the following action does, it separates my problems from their problems.

NAMING THE RESISTANCE IN A NEUTRAL WAY

In order to keep my own issues clear, I have to find some *neutral* way to get the problem on the table. I know from Sparks that blaming someone else will only put the solution further out of reach, so scapegoating is out. Instead, I might say, "I'm having trouble because the subject keeps changing. Can you help me stay focused on one thing at a time?" I've avoided saying that the *other person* is changing the subject; perhaps it is something I'm doing that I don't notice. Instead of making any accusations, I've stated *my* problem.

If I keep my statement neutral, I can draw more accurate conclusions from the response. For a situation in which the client keeps asking for endless details, I might say, "I believe we can make some progress on solving the problem without that information, so I'd like to propose that we try working for a while with what we have." This is a neutral statement of my perception of things, and is quite different from saying, "You don't really need all that information," which would be a statement of the client's needs—needs that I couldn't possibly know.

Waiting for a Response

Naming the resistance in a neutral way is a comment on the *process*, and changes the discussion to an entirely different plane from that on which the resistance is taking place. But keeping things on a neutral plane is the hardest part for me to do, because I must keep my mouth shut: I try to limit my statement to no more than two short sentences. Then I stop talking.

And I wait.

And I wait.

And sometimes I wait some more.

Waiting is hard for me because I get tense when the room grows silent. But so do the clients, and it's their problem we're working on, not mine. Eventually, I'll be gone from the scene, leaving them to implement the changes, so I might as well let them practice taking responsibility. They always do, eventually, if I wait long enough.

Dealing with Questions

Sometimes, the response simply takes another resistant tack. In that case, I simply repeat the process and eventually I find the client addressing the true concerns. I tend to get hooked, though, by the client who asks questions, even though it is often the same question but in slightly altered form. Asking questions is an easy way to control a consultant who is brimming with answers to anything and has a desperate need to be understood. In order to break this habit, I answer in good faith—but no more than three times. After that, I regard the questioning as a form of resistance and name it in a neutral way. I might say, "I've answered three questions, but I don't see the direction we're going in." Then I wait.

By naming the resistance in this way, I have, in effect, said, "We are not making the progress I think we could be making. What do you have to say about that?" When the clients finally comment, they will probably respond to what I have implied rather than what I have actually said. If they do, we have begun the process of finding the underlying source of the resistance, which the clients and I can do together.

LOCATING THE NATURE OF THE RESISTANCE

Having identified the resistance, I'm often tempted to rush right in to try to set things right. Most people have theories about how to overcome resistance, but most of those theories won't work for a consultant.

A Buffalo Story

I threw a party to introduce some of my friends to Morton, who owns a buffalo ranch with about two hundred head. My guests included Jack, a high-school math teacher; Mona, owner-manager of a public relations firm; and Wendy, a senior systems analyst in a hospital. Morton supplied the main course, but the charcoal fire was slow in starting. Soon everybody was grumbling about something or other.

"It's been a lousy week," Mona growled. "I can't seem to get anyone to work as hard as I do. I can't even make people come to work on time. Next week, I'm just going to have to crack down."

"You ought to be glad you're not a teacher," Jack said. "I'd like to crack down, but I'm so surrounded by rules I can't make the students do anything. Just once, I'd like to be able to take a birch rod to a few of those lazy ones."

Wendy laughed. "At least you have *some* authority. As a systems analyst, *nobody* has to listen to me, let alone do what I say. We spent a year building a new computer system, but the doctors and nurses just ignore it. If I could be in charge of that hospital for just one day, I'd *make* them use it."

I could appreciate their problems, but I don't think they could relate to mine when I told them, "It's much worse being an author. At least you're *there*, Wendy, so you have a chance to make the doctors and nurses do what you want. I write stuff and send it out into the world, after which time I have no control at all. If people don't want to read it, they just ignore it. Boy, I've written some great stuff that would really be influential, if only I could force a few crucial people to read it."

Just then, Dani gently reminded me that it was time to put on the buffalo burgers, so I didn't hear their reactions to *my* hard-luck story. I was kind of glad to get away, though, because it was getting rather depressing.

The Buffalo Bridle

Fortunately, the arrival of the buffalo burgers changed the focus of the conversation to Morton. "These are *delicious*," Mona said, dabbing with her napkin at a little trickle of burger juice on her chin. "But I've heard that it is really hard to raise buffalo in confinement."

"Yeah," Jack contributed, "didn't I read somewhere that buffalo won't stay penned up, that they go through barbed-wire fences like butcher's twine?"

"Don't need fences," Morton replied, "as long's you use the buffalo bridle."

"I don't believe I've ever seen a buffalo bridle. I suppose it must be very solidly made."

"Ain't *made* a'tall."

Jack looked even more puzzled than I felt. "I'm afraid I don't catch your meaning."

"It ain't somethin' you make. It's somethin' you *know*."

Now, I pride myself on knowing a lot of things, but concerning buffalo, I had no investment in my expertise, so I asked, "And what's that?"

"Well, if you're gonna control buffalo, you got to know two things, and only two things: First is,

"You can make buffalo go anywhere, just so long as they want to go there.

"And second,

"You can keep buffalo out of anywhere, just so long as they don't want to go there."

"I think *all* animals are like that," Wendy said, "but it's not so important to know that for *small* animals. They have to stay where they're put, or go where they're dragged."

Wendy had a point there, one I thought I might be able to use in an essay. In fact, something had happened just a few days earlier that perfectly illustrated Wendy's point about small animals. I settled back into my story-telling posture and told my tale.

A Dog Story

Dani and I had gone up to Omaha to give a seminar on the subject of "communication." To be sure of being well-rested, we took a room in the seminar hotel the night before. Unfortunately, just after we got into bed, a dog next door started whining and barking up a fit.

Being dog lovers, we couldn't simply ignore this poor beast, obviously abandoned in a strange room. I called the front desk and reported the situation.

"You must be mistaken," came the polite reply. "Dogs are not permitted in the rooms."

"So much the worse."

"What room do you think the dog is in?"

"I don't *think*, I know. It's in room 206."

Pause. "No, you're surely mistaken. There's nobody registered in room 206."

"Then you've got a freeloader or an abandoned dog."

"The dog must be outside. It should go away in a few minutes."

"Could you just send someone to check room 206, please!"

"Oh, all right! I'll send the engineer around when he gets finished."

I don't know what the engineer was doing, but he didn't finish for the next half hour. The dog was still whining, and we were still listening, so I called again. Again I was promised that the engineer would come, but nothing happened.

"They don't seem to *want* to believe us," Dani observed. "They're not going to do anything unless you go out there and make a fuss."

"If I go out there naked, they might pay some attention, but it's too cold. And if I get dressed, I'll never get back to sleep."

"Well, I don't see how we can make them come unless one of us goes out to the front desk and starts tearing the furniture apart."

"Eureka!" I shrieked, leaping from the bed, drier than Archimedes, but just as naked. I phoned the front desk. "This is Mr. Weinberg, in room 204. I'm calling about the dog, which is still barking."

"We've had the engineer check on that, Mr. Weinberg. There's no dog in room 206."

"Well, it may not be a dog, but I can hear *something* in there. And it seems to be going berserk. A while ago it was just barking, but now I can hear it . . . " I paused to sound like I was listening, " . . . tearing up the furniture."

"Oh? Really tearing up the furniture?"

"That's certainly what it sounds like from this side of the wall. . . . Yes, I can definitely hear wild ripping sounds. . . ."

"Mr. Weinberg, I'll call you back in a few minutes."

She never did call, but within thirty seconds we heard sounds of the dog being escorted out of room 206.

A People Story

"That certainly illustrates Wendy's point," Jack said when I had finished. "That dog didn't want to stay in there, and if it had been as big as a buffalo, it would have gone right through the wall."

Mona looked pensive. "I guess what Morton would have done was leave something in the room to keep the dog interested in staying. Like a toy, or another dog of the opposite sex."

"That's my secret," Morton said. "Of course, I don't know dogs the way I know buffalo, but I guess I could figger somethin' that would make the dog *want* to stay in the room."

"As I see it," Dani observed, "that's exactly what Jerry did to the desk clerk. Until he hit on something *she* wanted, he wasn't able to move her at all. Once he did, it was all over in less than a minute."

"Yeah," Jack said, "Jerry sure was lucky. Like Morton is lucky to be working with such docile animals. Too bad for me that high-school students aren't like buffalo. Teaching would be a snap if you could teach children anything you wanted to teach them just by making them want to learn it. But I've got all I can do just to get through the material my *principal* wants. Who has time to work on finding out what the *students* want?"

"I couldn't agree more," said Mona. "Maybe if people would work a little harder on *my* projects, I'd have some time to learn about *their* desires. But if they aren't going to do the company's work with any enthusiasm, what's the point of my spending time thinking about them?"

"I know how you feel," Wendy added. "If the doctors and nurses would only consider how bad I feel when they don't use my system, and appreciate how much I want them to like it and use it, maybe my job wouldn't be such a drag. But I just can't seem to get them to see my point of view."

Somehow, the conversation had drifted back to the depressing topic of work, but I couldn't resist being sucked in. "Well, an author's life would really be simple if people behaved like buffalo. All I'd have to do is relate what I have to say to what they are interested in. But very few people are interested in the right things, as far as I can tell. If they were, they'd gobble up my books the way you've gobbled up those buffalo burgers."

Morton nodded his agreement, slowly turning his head to stare at each of us in turn, first Jack, then Mona, then Wendy, then directly at me. "Yep. I sure am glad I work with buffalo. I never could understand people."

Work Together to Discover the Source

The Buffalo Bridle is the key to handling resistance. I can't apply it successfully when I'm more interested in what I want than in what my clients want. You'd think I could see that they're more interested in what they want than in what I want, but I frequently forget. Perhaps the difference between buffalo and people is that buffalo can learn from experience.

"Resistance" is the consultant's label. To the client, it is "safety." People do things because they think they will gain more than they will lose. They resist when they perceive a negative balance. Generally, such a balance is composed of many factors, some of which are gains and some are losses. In searching for the source of resistance, I work with the client to make a complete list of both. I'm always a bit scared I might bring up something negative that the client hadn't thought of, but the process of working with the client is more important than the list itself.

Working together brings subconscious factors into the light. Clients tend to overestimate negative factors that go unspoken. The best ghost-story writers never describe their monsters too explicitly, because the ghost you can see clearly is the ghost you can learn to live with. When my client and I put a name and a clear description on some potential loss, the irrational fear evaporates.

But most of the factors my clients forget are positive, including even ones that seem obvious to me. Sometimes, the benefits I perceive are of no importance to my client, while at other times, the client attaches much more importance to a benefit than I could imagine. It's not important what *I* think of the benefits. That's why I must make them public.

Find and Test Alternative Approaches

An excellent way to disclose the unconscious sources of resistance is by testing the attractiveness of alternative approaches. Typical probes might include

- "How would you feel if we stretched out the schedule by six months?"

- "Would this plan seem more attractive if we could somehow cut the cost by thirty percent?"

- "What if we could do it without bringing in additional people?"

- "Suppose we left the computer alone and changed just the manual procedures?"

- "What *one* thing could we change in this plan that would make the most difference to you?"

This last question can be powerful, but some clients are too rooted in "reality" to ask for something that they believe is impossible. Since we're not trying to solve the problem at this stage, but merely trying to identify the source of the resistance, we need to get the client unhooked from this stifling train of thought. Sometimes, we have succeeded with the following question: "If the Good Fairy granted you just one wish about this plan, what would it be?"

Introducing the explicit element of fantasy seems to unhook most people by making it clear that we're playing a game. At times, however, the conscious mind replies, "I just can't think of anything," when it's really saying, "My subconscious doesn't want to let you see the source of its resistance, because it's afraid you might find a clever way to overcome it."

At times I can circumvent the subconscious defenses by saying, "I know you can't think of anything you'd like to change about this plan, but if you could think of something, what would it be?" At least half the time, this paradoxical question gets right to the core of the matter. It does so because paradox is the language of the subconscious.

Another paradoxical way around the client's inability to identify the resistance is to emphasize the positive, by asking, for example, "What do you like *best* about this plan?" Once you have that answer, you can ask, "What do you like *next* best?" Eventually, certain aspects of the plan will become conspicuous by their absence.

PREVENTING RESISTANCE

You can also escape from a dead end by turning the whole emphasis around from change to constancy, that is, from what clients want to happen to what they *don't* want to happen: I ask a question such as, "As we implement this plan, what is the one thing you want to be sure doesn't change?"

If I remember to ask this question before I start rattling off plans for change, I may avoid resistance altogether. In fact, getting rid of resistance is merely doing the job I should have done in the first place, if I had understood my client better. Therefore, the same techniques can be used before or after the resistance actually arises.

Reducing Uncertainty

The most important word in the previous question is "sure." Probably ninety percent of resistance comes from uncertainty, which is reasonable because we are talking about the future. Nobody knows the future, and clients are usually wiser about this than consultants. People who are realistic about risks don't become consultants.

Resistance based on uncertainty can be overcome by techniques that reduce risk. That's why extending schedules is a universal balm for anxious clients, who know instinctively that time wounds all heels. At the first mention of granting more time to implement a change, all involved seem to sigh with relief—except for the person who's being pushed from the outside to make a deadline.

The desire for more time may be a specific need for time or a general need for reducing uncertainty. I can discover which it is by reducing uncertainties, such as the uncertainty about the precise details of the plan. I tend to work so intuitively that I often leave my dazed clients wondering just what the devil I'm talking about. One client recently brought me back to earth by asking, "That number 30—does it mean 30 people or $30,000?" If my communication was no better than that, no wonder he was resisting.

Once I've cleared away the uncertainties over what I'm talking about (which should never be underestimated), there always remains an irreducible residue of uncertainty. If this residue is still too much for my client to tolerate, I consider modifying the plan to include some form of insurance against the risks. Agricultural agents in developing countries sometimes offer such insurance to overcome the typical peasant farmer's resistance to trying a new technique. If the farmer agrees to use the technique, the agent guarantees to pay the farmer any difference between this year's and last year's income. If this year's income is better, the farmer pockets the surplus.

The insurance takes the form of "If your fear is realized, then thus-and-such will be done to make up for it." The alternative need not be in dollars and cents. One client relieved fears about joining a risky project by giving each participant a written guarantee of a specific job if the project was terminated prematurely. Another client gave participants vouchers that were good for specified amounts of company-paid training, which they could use for any courses they desired, whenever they desired. Both these devices ensured the participants that their personal losses would be less, even if the project proved unsuccessful.

Getting Out of the Way

In the end, the most important part of overcoming resistance is to prevent it from becoming frozen in place. That's why I must always avoid "resisting the resistance." I may win the argument, but I may also place the clients in a position where changing their mind is a form of "losing." The risk of losing face in the here-and-now always seems bigger than the risk of losing a million dollars in the there-and-then.

For me, the risk of losing face is even worse, because my "face" is my client's business and the million dollars at risk isn't my money. When a plan seems to be frozen in a state of resistance, chances are two-to-one that it's me who's frozen, not the client. That's why I keep returning to the process of identifying the source of resistance, starting with my own gut.

Once again, my purpose is to help the client to solve a problem, not to demonstrate my superior intelligence or dominant will. As a consultant, my involvement in my client's success or failure is minor at best, so I mustn't let myself be overcome by delusions of grandeur. Even so, I make mistakes.

When I can't get past the resistance, I try not to take it personally. Taking it personally merely guarantees that the client either will continue resisting, or will stop just to please me, which is precisely the wrong reason. When an impasse reaches a certain point, it's best simply to let go and announce, "I'm afraid this one is too big for me. I hope you'll solve it, but I can't think of anything else that might help you."

Each time I've managed to let go like that, I first resisted for an excessively long time. I was afraid that I would lose the client's respect, but the fear was, like most resistance, irrational. Each time this has happened, the client's respect for me has increased, because I showed I was powerful enough to admit that I wasn't omnipotent.

What amazes me most is that as soon as I let go, the client's resistance usually collapses. It's hard to resist when nobody's pushing.

11

marketing
your services

Spend at least one-fourth of your time doing nothing.
—The Ninth Law of Marketing

At a recent consultants' workshop, we were trading war stories on how we got started in the consulting business. Marty explained that he had been working as a computer programmer in North Carolina when his employer decided to move their headquarters to Philadelphia. He didn't want to move, but they needed his expertise to keep several systems running, so they offered to pay him his former salary for spending one week each month in Philadelphia. He had the rest of his time to himself, so he started looking for other clients.

Pamela was working as a trainer in a New York bank, conducting financial seminars for the bank's clients. The seminars gave her a chance to show her abilities to many client executives, and several of them asked her if she would be willing to help them improve their training programs. She left the bank and became an independent trainer and training consultant—with her former employer as her best customer.

HOW CONSULTANTS GET STARTED

Marty and Pamela are typical. Most consultants get into the business by accident. And most of them start with at least one major client already signed up. In this way, at least, consulting is a unique business. You wouldn't start a boutique or a garage or a restaurant or a health spa by accident.

The "approved" way to start a small business is to survey the market, then plan how to create a demand or meet existing market needs. Because most consultants start by accident, with bread and butter assured by their first client, they rarely give a thought to marketing their services—until they lose their first client. Then they come to me, ready to learn the laws of marketing.

THE LAWS OF MARKETING

The Right Amount of Business

The first thing I do is pose a riddle.

Question: How do you tell an old consultant from a new consultant?

Answer: The new consultant complains, "I need more busi-
             ness." The old consultant complains, "I need more
             time."

It is the consultant's lot to have either too much time and too little
business, or too little time and too much business, which leads us to The
First Law of Marketing:

**A consultant can exist in one of two states: State I (idle) or State B
(busy).**

For consultants, there are lots of free lunches, but there's no such thing
as "just the right amount of business."

I give this law first because it's essential for any consultant to
have realistic marketing goals. Consultants who started by accident
may temporarily have just the right amount of business, which gives
them a false impression of what consulting is like. I've never met a
consultant who consistently has exactly the right amount of business.
If your goal is to have a comfortable business, with just enough work
to keep you comfortable, buy a fish market or join the Army. Stay out
of consulting.

The Best Way to Get Clients

Why isn't it possible to have just the right amount of business? For
one thing, the amount of business you have partially determines the
amount of business you get. When a consultant asks me the best way to
get new clients, I must, in all honesty, reply with The Second Law of
Marketing:

The best way to get clients is to have clients.

Needless to say, this answer doesn't make them happy, because they're
in State I. If they already *had* clients, they wouldn't be asking for
marketing advice, but that's exactly the wrong timing. The time to look
for consulting business is when you have too much consulting business.

Everyone likes to go with a winner. There's no better marketing
tool than a sincere refusal to consider additional work. Because consultants spend a lot of time in State I, prospective clients see most consultants as overly eager to get work. If they happen to encounter you when
you're in State B, they decide you must be something special. They want
you for their consultant, and even if they can't have you right now,
they'll call you first when they have another assignment.

Exposure Time

Because the best way to get clients is to have clients, the rich get richer and the poor, poorer. Many of the poor consultants get discouraged and drop out of the business. Most of the rich ones, however, eventually make a mistake that drops them out of State B and back to State I.

For one thing, they're so busy in State B that they forget that State B is the best time to do marketing. The Third Law of Marketing is designed to remind them:

Spend at least one day a week getting exposure.

State I consultants have no trouble accepting this law; they have nothing better to do with their time. But State B consultants are too busy. If I do convince them that their business might drop some day, they respond by working harder—to squirrel away cash for the hard times to come.

What they fail to realize is that there are three kinds of exposure: the kind you pay for, the kind you get free, and the kind you get paid for. Advertising is exposure you pay for, and is of little interest to individual consultants. I've never known an independent consultant who got a dollar's worth of business from advertising.

The only essential advertising expense is for business cards and stationery so people will remember your address and phone number. You can distribute the business cards whenever you get free exposure, that is, in professional groups you join, at meetings you address, to people you meet on airplanes. If you're enterprising and committed to spending one day a week getting exposure, you'll have no trouble thinking of free opportunities.

If you're even more enterprising, you'll manage to get paid for getting exposure. If you cultivate your speaking skills, many groups will pay you to address them. If you polish your writing skills, there are hundreds of magazines hungering for articles. Just be sure they include your address. If you develop your training skills, you can conduct seminars in which people will pay to be introduced to your abilities.

Many consultants have found their promotional activities transformed into their main source of revenue. Even if that doesn't happen, the type of revenue provided by such activities tends to run on a different cycle from consulting revenues. I've noticed that when times are hard for the consulting business, my book royalties seem to rise. Perhaps a book is a pauper's consultant.

How Important Are You?

I must confess that I have a hard time swallowing the need to spend so much time getting exposure. I'm sensitive to rejection, and if I make a marketing effort, someone might say no. When business is good, I like to imagine it's because I'm such a good person, not because I've made any marketing effort. All I have to do is remain a good person and the business will remain good.

Because of my inability to face reality, I need a Fourth Law of Marketing that reminds me:

Clients are more important to you than you can ever be to them.

Some of my clients are businesses grossing more than ten billion dollars a year. If they give me ten thousand dollars' worth of work, I certainly appreciate it and they don't even notice it. One of these huge clients paid Dani's forty-four hundred dollar invoice twice. After several tries at getting someone to believe they had actually paid twice, Dani was told that it would be much simpler for everyone involved if she just kept the money. They were too big to handle such a small refund, but she was too small to keep it. She deducted it from their next bill.

I've had clients who, as they were cutting me out of their budget, sincerely told me that I was "the best consultant they had ever used." Someone upstairs had issued an edict to cut expenses by two-tenths of a percent, and no expense is easier to cut than an outside consultant. One polite letter is all it takes, or a phone call if you're pressed for time.

I have lost "solid" contracts for every imaginable reason outside of my own performance. One company moved my client's operation overseas. Another moved the manager overseas, and the new manager brought in his own consultant. One company discontinued my contract under a general move that cut all contracts under $5,000 (because they were too troublesome to administer). I would have raised my prices, but I found out too late. In each case, the client expressed great regrets, but none was as great as mine.

In other words, no matter how solid your business seems, you'd better follow the law that says to average one day a week getting exposure. Two telephone calls and a letter are all that stand between lunching at the Four Seasons and at the Salvation Army soup kitchen.

Big Clients

I have literally lost one-third of my business in a single day, with two phone calls and a letter. Other consultants have done even worse, losing *all* of their business with a single call. They had fallen into the most common of all consulting traps: that of letting one client get such a large share of their business that they could not survive the loss of that client. So, we always advise consultants to follow The Fifth Law of Marketing:

Never let a single client have more than one-fourth of your business.

There are a dozen ways to slip into an unhealthy dominance by one client. One way is to be an internal consultant, an employee. But even employees have several advantages over the external consultant whose business is one hundred percent with one client. They get employee benefits and a fair measure of job security. Even so, internal consultants should heed The Fifth Law and not allow themselves to get locked onto a single supporter in their organization.

Some consultants start their business with one client and never seek another. My friend Wesley was billing fifty percent of his time with many small clients when one of them suddenly offered him a full-time two-year contract. The prospect of doubling his income blinded him to the inevitable consequence of no work two years down the road when the contract expired. As could have been predicted, Wesley lost all other contacts during his full-time stint and was forced to take a job; he has never returned to consulting.

Arnold's experience was even more typical. He had six good clients, with a number of prospects in the background to replace any he lost. But just as one client stopped requiring his services, another asked him for more time. Now he had five clients; a few months later, the same thing happened, and he had four. Eventually, he was down to three. When the one that produced forty-five percent of his revenue dropped out, he couldn't survive. Now he's selling real estate.

Lynne's Law of Life

If Arnold had had more money in the bank, he might have survived this loss long enough to find another couple of clients, but like many consultants, he wasn't in the habit of saving money. Most people can continue indefinitely on three-fourths of their present income, which is why the law advocates no more than one-fourth to any one client. But financial reasons are not the whole story.

As Arnold crept slowly into the position of having fewer and fewer clients, each client became more critical. When one asked him for more of his time, he knew he should refuse, but he was afraid to lose that client's business altogether. Any time you're afraid to say no to your client, you lose your effectiveness as a consultant. You also lose the client's respect, which increases the chance that you'll eventually lose the business.

As my friend and consultant Lynne Grimes says,

> **"To be able to say yes to yourself as a consultant, be able to say no to any of your clients."**

This is far more important than a mere marketing law. I call it Lynne's Law of Life.

MORE LAWS OF MARKETING

Satisfied Clients

The Fifth Law of Marketing is *not* an admonition to throw clients away. Quite the contrary. By following it—and even more, by following Lynne's Law of Life—you ensure that you retain your clients' respect. This respect is essential because The Sixth Law of Marketing says

> **The best marketing tool is a satisfied client.**

For one thing, a previous client is twenty times better as a future prospect than somebody entirely new *if* you've done your job properly. But when you do try to sell yourself to somebody new, a specific reference triples your chances of landing the contract. That's why I always ask satisfied clients for permission to use them as references.

Such direct references, however, are the least important way my satisfied clients market for me. Client R called me because another client had gratuitously mentioned my name at a rugby match. Client S came to me because he had worked at another company seven years earlier when I had come to do a checkup. He had been impressed with the way I worked, and now that his department needed a checkup, he never even considered calling anyone else.

Dani once got an assignment by a doubly indirect reference. Client T gave her his business because another consultant recommended her. This consultant had worked with a former client of hers, and had heard such raves about her work that he gave Client T her name without hesitation.

I used to be puzzled by the number of calls I got that seemed to come out of the blue. In recent years, I've taken to asking callers how they got my name. It helps me to understand marketing (like the fact that ninety percent of my business now comes directly or indirectly from satisfied clients), but equally important, it also lets me thank the person who recommended me.

Giving It Away

But what are the best ways to get satisfied clients? Although there are dozens of ways, several are so commonly violated that it's useful to elevate them to the stature of laws of marketing.

First of all, it's necessary to observe that consulting is a high-risk business. One good idea can make you as rich as Midas, but a second good idea can transfer the golden touch to someone else and put you in the poorhouse. It's no business for cowards. As soon as you lose your nerve, you stop investing in new ideas and try to milk your last idea for the maximum return. But as soon as you lock onto a single idea, your days as a consultant are numbered. Ideas are too easy to steal.

One of the disadvantages of being in business for yourself is that sooner or later you'll have to deal with lawyers. Most employees don't have to deal with lawyers on business matters, but independent consultants do. Lawyers take some getting used to, but fortunately for me, my older sister Charlotte (Marvin's wife) is a lawyer, so I'm an authority on law without having to endure law school.

I must be an authority on law because consultants always ask me if they could sue a client for stealing one of their ideas. I always explain that although they can sue anybody they wish, the return on resources invested in new ideas is a thousand times greater than a similar investment in lawsuits. Lawsuits are tempting only when innovation is drying up. That's easy to see from the outside, but it doesn't feel good when it's your ideas that have been stolen. I feel genuinely robbed, cheated, and betrayed. And these angry feelings destroy my ability to keep innovating, so lawsuits seem the only reasonable alternative.

Once an important client copied an entire unpublished article of mine and printed it without a hint of credit. When I consulted Charlotte, she assured me that I had a perfect case in a court of law—and that I would be stupid to sue a good client.

Sometimes, the infraction is less clear: a case of someone copying an anecdote or diagram, perhaps with a few details changed; and sometimes, it's merely an idea, elaborated on and presented as original. Even so, my initial reaction is anger, and my impulse is to sue the bastards.

I've come to understand that my anger actually is a symptom of something else—a strong feeling of inadequacy. I'm afraid that I no longer have what it takes to turn out new ideas. Instead of reacting by creating a batch of new ideas, I start grasping for ways to protect the ones I've already produced. In short, I've lost my nerve.

I'm not ashamed to admit that I sometimes lose my nerve. When it takes all the running you can do to stay in the same place, it's no shame if you sometimes feel weary of running. Every consultant, at some time or another, has to face the feeling of wanting to stop and live off past glories. Each time that happens to me, I get frightened, and angry, and unable to produce new ideas. Then I rest for a while, do some new things, and eventually get back into the racket again.

I'm in the idea business, not the lawsuit business. My big payoff comes from generating new ideas, not hanging on to things that are done and gone. I remind myself that, as Aristotle said, "It is not once, nor twice, but times without number, that the same idea makes an appearance in the world." My ideas weren't original in the first place. I "borrowed" them from others and modified them in subtle ways.

Past glories are future graves. Instead of letting them bury me, I try to follow The Seventh Law of Marketing:

Give away your best ideas.

I do everything possible to encourage my clients to take over the work I've been doing. They usually give me direct credit, but even if they don't, they love me for my generosity. This increases the chance they'll give me future business, or recommend me to others.

The Duncan Hines Difference

It is possible, though, to destroy business by giving clients too much. Just after World War II, at the time packaged cake mixes were introduced, I was working in Hillman's Supermarket with Rudy and the rutabagas. I remember noticing that I never had to restock the cake mixes. The boxes just sat on the shelves, like the rutabagas, minding their own business. Gathering dust.

Then along came Duncan Hines. His name was renowned as a restaurant critic, and it seemed to work magic on a cake-mix box. As the dust deepened on the other brands, the Duncan Hines mixes required two or three restocks every day. Why should housewives be so devoted to a restaurant critic?

What Duncan Hines had done, I learned later, was appreciate the psychology of the housewife in a way that all his competitors had missed. Earlier mixes had emphasized convenience and simplicity: Nothing could be easier—all you had to do was add water and bake. But Hines realized that this was actually *too* easy. The average housewife felt degraded in her role as family baker when all she had to do was add water. It just wasn't *real* home baking.

So, Duncan Hines made it a little harder. With his mixes, you had to add an egg as well—a messy, slimy, gooey, yellow-and-white, honest-to-gosh egg! Lo and behold, that egg somehow involved the housewife in the cake, something that simply adding water couldn't accomplish. When she presented it to the family after supper, she could truthfully answer, "Yes, I baked it *myself!*"

What Duncan Hines discovered was The Eighth Law of Marketing, also called The Duncan Hines Difference:

It tastes better when you add your own egg.

The "egg" that makes the difference can be almost anything, as long as it's something consumers contribute for themselves.

The greeting card people have refined The Duncan Hines Difference to the point that all the consumer has to contribute is a *decision.* In the card commercials, Mother says, "Gee, Tommy, did you choose this card all by yourself? For me?" Tommy beams, just as much as he would have if he had painted the picture and written the poem. He chose it, so it's his card.

The Duncan Hines Difference explains why consultants who need business badly often drive their clients away. Any time I'm over-eager to sell myself, I try to have an answer to every question. Ignoring The Duncan Hines Difference, I stifle my clients' attempts to participate in solving their own problems. If I fail, I look stupid, which is bad enough. If I succeed, I make the client feel stupid, which is far worse.

Doing Nothing Is Doing Something

So here I am, trying to give you complete advice about marketing, which Dani reminds me is in direct violation of The Eighth Law. So, let me leave you room for an egg—The Ninth Law of Marketing:

Spend at least one-fourth of your time doing nothing.

By "nothing" I mean that you should not be doing anything that is billable to any client, you should not be out getting exposure, and you should not be doing administrative work at the office. Whatever else you do with that time is your own choice, and is the egg that makes you love my advice.

Why is doing nothing an important marketing tool? Here are some of my reasons, although you will have to add your own:

- If your time is solidly booked, you will not be in a position to take advantage of a sudden opportunity for new business.

- Although you don't want to jump in response to every command from your present clients, it is an important part of your service to be able to respond quickly to a genuine emergency.

- As a human being, you are subject to failures, like blizzards and broken legs, that might prevent you from keeping promises if you have no slack in your schedule.

- You are your only product: Without slack time to re-plenish yourself, you will soon either burn out or run out of fresh ideas. Either way, you won't sell.

- Practice at doing nothing will help you learn not to give your clients too much.

But can you afford to take so much time doing "nothing"? You certainly can, if you're an employee or have lots of employees to earn money for you. If you work for yourself, you can't—unless you price your services properly.

Let's do a very rough calculation. If you allot one-quarter of your time to marketing and one-quarter to slack, your billable time is only half your actual time. Continuing with the calculation, figure that you'll spend about half of what you earn on administrative expenses, and that you'll need an additional twenty percent as a contingency reserve, giving you a billing rate of about five times your target salary. That is, if you want to net $5 an hour over the whole year, you have to bill at an hourly rate of $25. If you want to earn $200 a day, you have to bill $1,000.

If you don't think you can sell yourself with a five times multiplier, then you're in the wrong business because if you bill at less than that, you'll soon be out of business anyway.

MARKETING FOR QUALITY

Here, then, is a review of the first nine laws of marketing:

1. A consultant can exist in one of two states: State I (idle) or State B (busy).

2. The best way to get clients is to have clients.

3.   Spend at least one day a week getting exposure.

4.   Clients are more important to you than you can ever be
     to them.

5.   Never let a single client have more than one-fourth of
     your business.

6.   The best marketing tool is a satisfied client.

7.   Give away your best ideas.

8.   It tastes better when you add your own egg.

9.   Spend at least one-fourth of your time doing nothing.

These laws tell you how to get new clients and how to retain the clients
you already have. If you apply the laws successfully, you will have too
much business: State B. Because of this business, you will tend to do a
poor marketing job, until you are back in State I. If these were the only
laws of marketing, you would be condemned, like Sisyphus, to an
eternally frustrating cycle of up and down.

     My sister Charlotte struggled for many years to be a lawyer, then
a successful lawyer, then a State B lawyer. One day, a client (the
husband in a lucrative divorce case) gave her an inventory of communal
property and how it was to be divided. Reading the list, her eye caught
on this item:

     Description: Joy dishwashing liquid, medium-size
     Condition: One-third full
     Location: Under kitchen sink
     Disposition: Husband

In that moment, Charlotte decided never to handle another divorce case.

     Like Charlotte or anyone else starting out in business, we have so
far been working under the assumption that the purpose of marketing is
to get more business. Although this may be true for the beginner, the
experienced consultant has a different perspective, as expressed in The
Tenth Law of Marketing:

     Market for quality, not quantity.

I call this Charlotte's Law, and it may be more important than all of Marvin's Great Secrets of Medicine and the other nine marketing laws combined. Whether you're a lawyer, an organizational consultant, or a technical expert, you will eventually reach either State I or State B. If you remain in State I for long, you'll be driven out of the business. But if you remain in State B, you'll find yourself getting rich. But for most rich people, money is boring.

One day, some partially filled bottle of Joy will snap you out of your preoccupation with marketing for more money. In a twinkling, you're going to ask yourself, "Is this all there is?" In that moment, your marketing question will be transformed from "How do I get more business?" to "Do I really want to do this?"

From there, it's but a tiny step to "How do I get to do things that are truly worth doing?" And strange as it may seem, these laws of marketing will do an even better job of making you happy than of making you rich.

12

putting a price on your head

If they don't like your work, don't take their money.
—The Sixth Law of Pricing

Oscar Wilde once said that people know the price of everything and the value of nothing. Since Wilde's time, however, things have gone downhill. Now people don't even know their own price. Not consultants, anyway. There may be some consultants in the world who never wonder whether they've set the right price on their heads, but I've never met any.

Such universal curiosity makes price an essential topic for a book directed at consultants, but there is a danger in approaching the subject directly because many consultants believe that thinking about money cheapens them. The danger to me of course is that by discussing price, I might lose readers. It just might be permissible to give a mechanical formula like "five times your desired hourly wage," but to offer more advice on pricing than that would definitely be in poor taste.

However, having gone this far with the book, I suppose it's too late to worry about poor taste. So, slip this book into a plain brown wrapper and read on, because the sections that follow are full of rules on that most tasteless of all subjects: the price of consulting.

SEX AND THE FIRST LAW OF PRICING

I grew up in the Midwest, but left to live in California. That was a long time ago, but I still remember the shock. Aside from the ocean and the weather and the traffic and the smog, the most shocking thing was the way people dealt with taboo subjects—like my next-door neighbor, Greta, for example. What I couldn't hear of her sex life through the plasterboard walls, Greta openly discussed on the front porch. But that wasn't the half of it. Greta worked for a cosmetics firm and was fond of revealing secrets of the "skin trade," as she called it. I remember the day she burned my ears with a story about pricing policies. In the Bible Belt, nice people just don't talk about such things.

Greta's story concerned a new lipstick her firm had introduced into variety stores all over the country. Priced competitively at one dollar, it was a dismal failure. The lipstick was withdrawn, but there was an enormous inventory already manufactured on which her firm would have to take a loss. Then, someone had the bright idea of raising the price to five dollars so the lipstick would be marketed in fancier stores. The ploy was an immediate success, selling out the entire inventory in two weeks.

183

Why are people so fascinated with pricing? Like sex, price setting is done behind closed doors, consumes a lot of energy, and has unpredictable consequences. But one of the reasons sex fascinates us is that it can mean so many things to so many people, all at the same time. It's a means of procreation, an expression of love, a method of gaining power and control, a physical exercise, an exciting game of chance, a business deal, a confirmation of self-worth, and a great deal of pleasure in and of itself. Except for the physical exercise, most of the same things can be said about the prices consultants set on their services. Hence, The First Law of Pricing:

Pricing has many functions, only one of which is the exchange of money.

As we'll see, if you focus on the money aspects, you'll probably set the wrong price.

IMAGE AND THE SECOND LAW OF PRICING

Lipstick that won't sell at one dollar may sell enormous quantities at five dollars, which is exactly the kind of psychology that works for some consultants. You're sending your clients a mixed message if you bill yourself as the world's foremost authority and charge minimum wage. They're going to go through all the trauma of bringing in an outside consultant, violating all their instincts and all their ego gratification needs, and the very least they'll want is ego-boosting reassurance that they're getting the best possible consultant. There's no way they could get the best possible consultant for minimum wage. Or, so they think, because as The Second Law of Pricing states,

The more they pay you, the more they love you.

Within a certain range, the higher your price, the more business you get. Eventually, of course, too high a price will prevent clients from retaining you. Even though they'll love you, you won't get the business.

You can lower your fees to get business, but don't forget that there's another way of stating this Second Law of Pricing:

The less they pay you, the less they respect you.

Once in a while, I agree to do some charity work, like giving a lecture at a university. These free, speaking engagements invariably require twice as much work and ten times the hassle as engagements that pay double my usual fees. Before the lecture, at least three different people from the university will call me with detailed information about just what I'm to do when I'm on campus—and all three give me different assignments. When I finally get my responsibilities clarified and ask my sponsor to confirm the details in writing, the confirmation arrives at the last minute and invariably changes the agreement. Over the years, I've become convinced that universities and other nonprofit organizations devote two-thirds of their staff to making sure that the other one-third is never exposed to the germ of a fresh idea. As an outsider carrying ideas that haven't been sterilized by years of working in this antiseptic environment, I'm especially threatening.

In contrast, when an organization offers me an exceptionally high price, my contact invariably says, "Do whatever you like. We'll be happy with whatever you give us." Because the price is so high, my clients believe that I know best what they ought to have. And because I'm obviously such an important person, they arrange all details quickly, clearly, and conveniently.

These observations suggest that price serves as an important screening device, and this generally is the case. When you ask for what you think you're worth and your prospects tell you the fee is too expensive, you can be sure that they won't respect you if you come down to their price. But that is not the only problem: Because such prospects don't believe you're worth your fee, they'll fill every moment of your time with planned busywork. When you arrive, you'll receive a bland reception that is disappointing in and of itself, but more important, it generally is an indicator that the client will never do anything you suggest. So, in a way, the prospects are right: You *aren't* worth very much—to them. That's why you shouldn't work for clients who won't pay your regular price.

MORE THAN MONEY: THE THIRD LAW OF PRICING

Suppose you want to work with an organization that really has no possibility of meeting your usual fee scale. Don't let The Second Law discourage you: You can still make the client respect you by setting the proper price. All you need to remember is The Third Law of Pricing:

The money is usually the smallest part of the price.

The Third Law is especially important to the *internal* consultant, making it possible for the employee on a fixed wage to be respected as much as any high-priced outside authority.

If you examine the total "cost" to a client of using your services, you'll find that there are many costs besides the money. There is the psychological cost of admitting there is a problem, the labor to get approval for your visit, the difficulty of changing schedules, the time and trouble to line up people to see you, plus all the extra work the client might have to do after you've gone.

By arranging for clients to pay something that's of value *to them*, even if it's not paid to you, you have, in effect, raised the price. If they've invested something in getting you there, then they'll pay attention to you once you arrive. The other side of this coin is that you may inadvertently raise the price beyond what the clients are willing to pay, even though not much money changes hands.

ALTERNATIVE FEES: THE FOURTH LAW OF PRICING

Knowing that price is more than money, you can increase your compensation in a variety of ways that may not increase the cost to your client. As an author, I often increase my income from a visit by selling my own books. As a consultant, I can sometimes use services such as arranged contacts with prospective clients in the area, computing services, or the use of a library. Many of these benefits are also available to the internal consultant, and are especially valuable to someone on a fixed wage.

As a tourist, I often get free travel to a place I've always wanted to visit. When I can arrange a day off or a weekend, I frequently ask my clients to take me sightseeing around their area. We all have a lot of fun and improve our relationships, and I learn some geography in the bargain. Universities are particularly good at this. They'll usually provide a couple of graduate students to take you around. Graduate students are a more interesting lot than professors and generally know the most interesting places to visit.

If you plan it right, a visit to a university can be very rewarding professionally, far in excess of any fee. If you don't plan it right, you'll just be used, wrung dry of whatever knowledge you have, treated with disrespect or ignored, and then cast aside to find your own way back to the airport swearing never to go back to a university again.

I look upon my consulting as a way of getting a paid education, and where better to do that than in a university? By arranging visits with good people, I get the best that a university has to offer, without the excess baggage. The curious thing is that most people consider these visits an extra benefit, rather than an extra cost, which illustrates The Fourth Law of Pricing:

Pricing is not a zero-sum game.

In other words, my gains don't have to be their losses. By searching for conditions that benefit us both, I can lower the effective price without lowering my image in their eyes, thus beating the law that says they'll respect me less if I charge a lower price. For instance, universities can sometimes provide a specialized audience on which I can test new material. I see members of this audience as experimental subjects, but they see themselves as participating in the leading edge of knowledge.

Sometimes, the clients can literally be experimental subjects, for example, as participants in a survey I'm taking. When they're not paying my usual fee, I feel justified in asking them to be experimental subjects, although even the people who pay my full fees are usually more than happy to be participants, too. In fact, I can even arrange to incorporate *all* these extra "benefits" in my consulting assignments with clients who are paying full fees; they're so happy to have me there, they do what I ask without any hesitation. Besides, there are added benefits for them, too.

NEED FOR MONEY AND THE FIFTH LAW OF PRICING

All of this illustrates that in order to set fees properly, you have to start from a base of knowing what you're trying to accomplish with your fee. One thing that most people think of when setting fees is that they're trying to make a living. This is a big mistake, and violates The Fifth Law of Pricing:

If you need the money, don't take the job.

Why not? If you need money badly, you may set your price too high in order to try to get solvent on this one job. Or, you may set your price too low, hoping to sell the job on the basis of price. Both of these occurrences destroy the usefulness of price as a tool in your consulting.

In any case, if you really need the job that badly, you're not likely to get it because when you negotiate with the client, your anxiety is going to show. The client will reason, probably with some justification, that a consultant who needs business that badly can't be very good. And don't kid yourself. It always shows. Ask any real estate dealer. Your clients may not be able to articulate just what it is that bothers them, except to say that you didn't inspire confidence. Or, that you didn't seem very authoritative. But clients always know.

Things are no better even if you actually sell the job. Suppose you set your price too high in hopes of a big payoff. Then, because you realize the price is too high, you may start making exaggerated claims on the kind of service you're going to be able to provide. If you price the job too low and sell it, the sale won't take care of your financial problems. So, the next time, you'll be in that much more trouble.

If you're desperate for business, the best strategy may be to offer your services free. Be nice and up-front about the fact that you're just starting out and you have a lot to learn, so that you aren't trying to hide anything. Some clients will appreciate this openness and give you a chance.

Another possible deal is to offer your services on the basis of a fee that will be paid only if your client is completely satisfied with your work. This is the policy I always use, although I express it in a more positive way. Any time I do work, I explain that after we're finished, if my clients don't agree that it was worth the fee, they can have their money back.

It's difficult to negotiate such a contingency fee if you really need the money. That is, it's difficult to make the offer in a sincere way. You will be tempted not to mention your guarantee, but if you do mention it sincerely, you will inspire a certain amount of confidence.

Even more important, you'll inspire your own confidence in yourself. After you've done the job, if the client doesn't ask for the money back, you know you must have reached some minimum level of performance. If you've negotiated the contract right, and if you've done your job properly, you ought to have some direct feedback on your performance. But there's something about the reality of a fee, a contingency fee, as feedback that surpasses all the evaluation forms that you might concoct. For that reason, if for no other, I subscribe to The Sixth Law of Pricing:

If they don't like your work, don't take their money.

Price is more than money, but it's also true that

Money is more than price.

This Seventh Law of Pricing means that you can use the exchange of money to create the conditions you need in order to be successful at consulting. For instance, when clients want me to hold a certain date, I may ask for a nonrefundable fee to compensate for possible loss of business if they change their mind. Such a fee also forces clients to consider the contract more carefully, and to respect the value of my time.

If my first face-to-face visit is to be far in the future, the client may not do any preparation until I actually arrive. To counteract this, I can set an advance-payment clause, which usually motivates people, and gets them working. Once a fee has been paid, people feel that the job has actually started, and they're more likely to buckle down and do what I suggest.

If the client has asked me to do a job that I'm not certain I can do, I may set my fees in stages. This gives both of us a way to cancel out as the project develops, without considering cancellation a failure. The first stage of such a project might be an estimated five percent of the total cost, after which time we will consider what we should do next in the light of what has been accomplished. Setting a staged fee communicates to the client that I am not sure I understand the problem. In such cases, the first stage is usually one of problem definition. Most clients realize that if I don't know what the problem is, I can't quote a price.

NEGOTIATION AND THE EIGHTH LAW OF PRICING

We've already seen that pricing is not something you can do in isolation, but The Eighth Law of Pricing makes that implication a bit more explicit:

Price is not a thing; it's a negotiated relationship.

For almost any consultant, an investment of a few dollars in a good book on negotiation will pay for itself a hundred times over. In my case, it paid off even more when I gave the book and the responsibility for negotiating my contracts to Judy, my office manager. Judy intrinsically is a better negotiator than I am. Even more important, she finds it easier to put a high value on my services than I do. This exudes an air of confidence to my clients and, incidentally, earns me fees that are ten to twenty percent higher than I would be comfortable asking for myself.

Having Judy negotiate also means that all agreements are scrupulously recorded and exchanged with the client. This practice prevents misunderstandings. When I negotiate for myself, I forget to write things down or follow up in writing. Judy never fails to do this and her diligence has saved me untold amounts of trouble and misunderstanding.

Dealing through Judy has also helped me to make my feelings and assumptions about fees explicit. When I'm offered a new kind of work, Judy and I sit down to discuss setting a fee. This process forces me to think out loud. It also forces me to take a little time before coming to some hasty decision that I may well regret later.

Through discussions with Judy, I arrived at the principle by which I now set all fees in new situations. I call this Ninth Law of Pricing my Principle of Least Regret:

Set the price so you won't regret it either way.

When I set a fee, there are two possibilities: One is that the client will accept it, I'll do the work, and I'll be paid that fee; the other is that the client will reject it, I won't do the work, and I won't get that fee. The Ninth Law says that I should set the fee so that whatever happens, I'll feel more or less the same.

To apply The Ninth Law, I must know my feelings about money, time, travel, and varieties of work. For example, suppose a client offers me a problem in which I'm only moderately interested. Suppose further that I recently worked on a similar problem and charged $5,000. I recall that on that previous job I was rather bored and felt sorry I had taken the work.

On the basis of those memories, I might raise my price for the current job to $7,500. If the client accepts and I reach the point of boredom, I can say to myself, "Well, at least I'm getting an extra $2,500 for doing this. That means I can take a couple of days off when I get back from this job. So, it's worth it." If the client turns down my offer, I can console myself by thinking, "Well, I know that if I took this job for less money, I would have regretted the whole thing before I was through."

Whenever I'm turned down for a job and then regret my high price, I try to make a mental note so that on the next similar job, I'll shave the price a little. But if I'm turned down and don't regret it, I leave the price alone. Eventually, I reach a stable price for a certain type of work—a price at which I'm happy to work, but below which I would be unhappy.

Of course, I always set the price so as not to destroy the price as an effective consulting tool. No matter how badly I want a job, I never lower my price below the level at which my client will respect me and listen to me. I know that if I do the job and I'm not effective, I'll regret it no matter how much money is involved. Similarly, if I charge too much, I know that I'll be unhappy because I'll feel that I'm not able to deliver something of value equal to what is being paid. Too high a price might make me push too hard for results that aren't really possible to obtain. This will destroy my consulting effectiveness, and when I'm not effective, I'm not happy.

FEE AS FEELING: THE TENTH LAW OF PRICING

The previous section may sound overly analytical, but I don't perform this balancing act in any particularly analytical way. I just lay out several prices in a range and than imagine myself in a situation in which I'm turned down and am sitting at home, or the situation in which I've accepted and I'm doing the job. As I imagine myself in each of these situations, I notice my feelings. I find these fantasy feelings a particularly reliable guide to how I'm going to feel in the actual situation. Based on where I feel best on all sides, I set my price.

If the procedure sounds fuzzy, you may want to review the pricing laws:

1. Pricing has many functions, only one of which is the exchange of money.

2. The more they pay you, the more they love you. The less they pay you, the less they respect you.

3. The money is usually the smallest part of the price.

4. Pricing is not a zero-sum game.

5. If you need the money, don't take the job.

6. If they don't like your work, don't take their money.

7. Money is more than price.

8. Price is not a thing; it's a negotiated relationship.

9. Set the price so you won't regret it either way.

If you examine these laws, you'll realize that they don't talk about rationality, but emotionality. In other words, underlying all the other laws of pricing is The Tenth Law:

All prices are ultimately based on feelings, both yours and theirs.

It's important to note other feelings, such as how strongly the clients feel their need, and what they feel they can pay. It's especially important to understand what they feel you're worth. But most important is what *you* feel you're worth.

In the case of consultants, Wilde was wrong. Consultants have so much trouble talking about prices because they know their value only too well. Or, they secretly fear that they know. So, if you're having problems setting a price on your head, take a good look at your deep feelings of self-worth. You're probably not worth as much as you hoped. On the other hand, you're probably worth a lot more than you feared.

13

how
to be trusted

Nobody but you cares about the reason you let another person down.
—The First Law of Trust

The Laws of Pricing tell us that price sets the conditions of work, but generally doesn't determine whether or not you get the job. Consultants are not commodities. One pork-belly might be pretty much like any other, but it's the differences between consultants that determine who gets the job. And who keeps it. Some people think that the most intelligent consultants get the most work, but there are many counter-examples.

IMAGE AND THE FIRST LAW OF TRUST

Take the case of Jack, a super-intelligent consultant who had difficulty keeping commitments. Because we shared some clients, I was occasionally held responsible for his unreliable behavior. After a particularly bad incident, I confronted him about his erratic behavior. He promised me he would be different next time, but I refused to accept his word. "Don't you trust me?" he asked.

"Frankly, no," I replied. "Why should I? You've lied to me so many times in the past."

"But I've *never* lied to you. It's just that unexpected things came up, so I couldn't deliver what I promised."

"All right, I can accept that. So you're not a liar."

"Then you'll trust me?"

"No way! What does it matter to me if you're a liar or are just incompetent? Or even just unlucky? I still can't trust you to deliver your half of the bargain."

Price Versus Trust

Jack was a nice guy. Jack was a competent consultant. Much of the time, our mutual work was advantageous to both of us. But each of his occasional lapses cost me more than I benefitted from twenty of his good jobs, and even when he was doing a good job, I couldn't get the fear of failure out of my mind. Working with Jack, I felt vulnerable, powerless to protect myself. That's why I ended our relationship.

Something similar often happens to the relationship between clients and consultants. According to Sherby, people usually feel weak and vulnerable when they retain a consultant. Small wonder that the

195

consultants they retain are first and foremost the ones they feel will not hurt them. Consultants who are looking for work should think less about price and learn more about *trust.*

The Value of Explanations

Looking back on our relationship, I really believe that Jack never understood why I didn't trust him. The fact that he spent so much time trying to convince me that he wasn't a liar indicates to me that he never comprehended that whether he was lying didn't matter to me at all. Of course, it mattered to *Jack:* The label of incompetence was only a slur on his ability, but calling him a liar was an attack on his integrity. Besides, Jack didn't really think he was incompetent. He thought he was just a solid, honest guy surrounded by liars, incompetents, and bad luck.

It's not unusual for people to be confused about trust, especially about why people don't trust them. One definition of trust is, "Firm reliance on a person's integrity or ability." Because the word mixes two different areas of trust, it's difficult to interpret the statement, "I don't trust you." It could mean "I can't rely on your ability," or it could mean "I can't rely on your honesty." But in all cases, it means "I can't rely on you."

In order for people to work effectively with me, they need an image of what I can do and what I can't do. If this image isn't accurate, the work won't go well. The same is true for my *self*-image, with one important difference. If I don't work well with someone, we don't have to continue to work together, but I'm stuck with myself—and my self-image—for life. I may be a jerk, but I'm the only jerk I have. That's why it's so important to me to retain a favorable self-image, even at the expense of the truth. And that's why whenever I let somebody down, I feel an urgent need to explain.

To me, this need to explain feels like something I'm doing for other people, to help them form an accurate image of me. That's why it's so hard to accept the idea expressed as The First Law of Trust:

Nobody but you cares about the reason you let another person down.

Other people can form all the image they need from deeds, not words.

FAIRNESS AND THE SECOND LAW OF TRUST

Any time a consultant acts in an unpredictable manner, the client's "firm reliance" may be eroded. Over the years, whenever I acted in a manner that appeared unreliable to my client, I usually lost the business.

Long before I understood why it was true, I had learned from bitter experience The Second Law of Trust:

Trust takes years to win, moments to lose.

It never seemed fair to me not to get a second chance to be trustworthy, especially since I had such excellent reasons for letting the client down. Eventually, I realized that I'm the same way when I'm on the other side. If you don't think you're the same, imagine putting your money in a bank that advertised: "We've only gone broke once," or rehiring an employee who says, "I only robbed you once."

Clients may lose their money, their jobs, or their reputation on the basis of the consultant's behavior. The ease with which they stop trusting you is the clients' instinctive way of increasing the consultant's risk, so that it will be commensurate with their own. Knowing this places a great incentive on the consultant not to make mistakes, whether of ability or integrity.

LOST TRUST AND THE THIRD LAW

Although the client will never listen to your reasons for being unreliable, you can be considered unreliable for failing to listen to the client. I had a client Dewey who explained to me that I was not to interview Fran, one of his employees. At the time, I was concentrating on what I wanted to do, so I didn't really hear Dewey's quarantine. When, in all innocence, I interviewed Fran, Dewey inferred that I was "sneaking around" his organization. To Dewey, I was dishonest. To me, I was an incompetent listener.

I learned about Dewey's inference years later, quite by accident. The reason I didn't learn about it directly was that Dewey never invited me back to his organization, and never told me why. His behavior was in complete accord with The Third Law of Trust:

People don't tell you when they stop trusting you.

After all, if the clients don't trust you, why should they bother communicating with you?

This unwillingness to communicate makes it very difficult for a consultant to correct behavior that the client sees as untrustworthy. If the consultant's problem is not listening, as mine was, then the problem is doubly difficult. Since that time, I've taken a number of steps to ensure that I hear the client. First, I have worked on my listening skills, both verbal and nonverbal. Second, whenever possible, I work with a partner so at least one of us can pay full attention to the listening problem. And third, I always contract in advance for a follow-up interview in which the client is expected to give me information about *my* performance.

TRICKS AND THE FOURTH LAW OF TRUST

But what if I had heard Dewey and still wanted to interview Fran? I might have approached the problem indirectly, perhaps manipulating the situation so that I encountered Fran by accident. This would have given me an alibi in case Dewey found out about the interview—and in case he bothered to ask me for an alibi. More likely, he would have said nothing and simply concluded (correctly, as it turns out) that I was a devious person and not to be trusted. I would lose his business and, because he'd never explain, always wonder why.

Like most people, I've always known that trust was crucial to human interaction, so for many years I searched for the secret tricks of being trusted. Before each new consulting assignment, I would concoct intricate plans for manipulating the client's feelings about me, none of which ever seemed to work. Eventually, I reached the point where I was unable to dream up anything new, so I asked Dani if she had any favorite tricks for building trust. "Sure," she said. "Try being straight for a change."

In a twinkling, my search was ended, for Dani had given me the one secret trick of being trusted, which is The Fourth Law of Trust:

The trick of earning trust is to avoid all tricks.

Using Dani's "trick," I would confront Dewey's prohibition in as forthright a manner as I could manage, as soon as it came up. I might tell Dewey, "You've retained me to learn as much as I can about your organization, so I'm concerned about any limit on me that might lower my effectiveness. I'm sure you have a good reason for forbidding me to interview Fran, and it would help me if you could explain it."

What I would do next depends on Dewey's reply. In two recent jobs, I was forbidden to see people for almost completely opposite reasons, yet the forthright approach worked in both cases. Let me consider them in turn.

In the first case, Ronald, the boss, replied, "Mike's too busy with super-critical work to spend the time with you. It would kill our project if he took an hour away from his work just now."

"Well," I said to Ronald, "if Mike's work is indeed so critical, I can see why you're so nervous about me taking his time. Rather than interviewing Mike, I think we should explore the reasons you're in such a situation. After all, even if I don't interview Mike, he might get the flu and have to go home an hour early. Does that really mean your whole project will collapse?"

In the second case, another boss, Shirley, told me, "Paul's an entirely negative person. If you listen to him, you'll get the impression that everything I do is utterly wrong."

I replied, "I've known people like that, Shirley, and you're right: They can contaminate an entire organization. I don't understand, though, why you keep Paul here, undermining your organization, if he's entirely negative. Perhaps we should work on the question of why you haven't removed him?"

Although the situations seem entirely opposite, my two replies share a common approach: I have shifted the focus away from the third party and brought the manager's reasoning into focus. Why? First of all, forbidding anything is a very strong action, indicating that the boss has intense feelings somehow connected with the employee. Second, if I don't understand the client's reasoning, *any* action I take is likely to appear unpredictable. If I act unpredictably on a matter involving intense feeling, I will certainly destroy my client's trust.

Getting hidden feelings out in the open is the most straightforward thing I can do to increase trust. In both of these cases, it allowed me to move quickly to the organization's most important problems.

WHO'S LYING? THE FIFTH LAW OF TRUST

Notice that I was careful not to agree with the manager's assessment of the facts in either case. I can agree that "if that is the case, I can see why you feel that way," but I must suspend judgment on the facts, which so far I know only through the manager. Half of trust is based on my honesty, but the other half is based on my *ability*. If I take unconfirmed opinions as fact, I'll never be a trustworthy consultant, even if I'm as honest as the President of the United States.

In disagreeing with clients, however, I must make it clear that I trust their *integrity*, even though I must reserve judgment on their *ability* to get the facts straight. I can get facts wrong myself, so it's reasonable to expect that other people can, too. Most people can accept the idea that even though they are sure of some fact, you, as a consultant and an outsider, need to find out for yourself. If they strongly resist this perfectly reasonable idea, then their resistance itself is an important fact that you should examine before going further. Why? Because they might be lying? But isn't that mistrusting their integrity?

I used to believe that clients lied to me when they gave me incorrect facts. When I was very young, I even made the mistake of accusing clients of lying, which was the end of any effective consulting relationship. Now I understand that very few people tell lies to consultants. They may intentionally give incorrect facts, but they never consider them lies, which leads us to The Fifth Law of Trust:

People are never liars—in their own eyes.

When I discover that someone has given me incorrect facts and I confront the issue, I am usually told something along the following lines:

- "I thought it would make it easier for you if I simplified the explanation in that way."
- "I felt it would cause trouble to allow you to investigate that problem, so I smoothed it over."
- "I knew that was irrelevant, so I simply omitted it to keep you from going on a wild-goose chase."

None of these actions—simplifying, smoothing, or omitting—are thought to involve lies. I act in a similar fashion when presenting data to people who are trying to deal with a complex situation, reasoning that it will help them reduce the amount of data to be handled. I'm up-front about the situation, so if the clients want more information, they can always ask for it.

I'm not trying to protect people from the effects of change—that would violate Rhonda's Third Revelation—but only from the effects of information overload. I sometimes make a mistake and fail to give needed information, but I recognize that it's equally wrong to overload people so they miss the important information. I certainly don't think of myself as lying, so if someone accuses me of lying, I stop trusting that person. I think my clients react the same way.

PROTECTION AND THE SIXTH LAW OF TRUST

I always believe that my clients are telling me the truth—as they see it, and as they think it would help me to hear it. I trust the clients' integrity, but I don't have to trust their ability. In other words, The Sixth Law of Trust is based on The Dealer's Choice:

Always trust your client—and cut the cards.

Pandora's Pox says that when your relationship with the client is new, it won't work. Experience tells me that at the very least, your early communications will be unreliable, so you need to protect yourself from communication failures.

"Cutting the cards" takes care of the clients' mistakes (or my mistakes in listening), but what if the clients really *are* lying? What if they are really trying to mislead me? Because I never rely on the *ability* of a single person to give me the truth, the whole truth, and nothing but the truth about a complex situation, lying presents no real problem. I routinely check any important fact from several different directions, so unless the entire organization is lying, I'll generally arrive at a true picture in the end.

If my final picture seems to contradict what someone told me, I always try to go back to that person and say, "In my notes, I recorded that you said thus-and-so, but from other sources I've found this-and-that. Can you help me reconcile the difference?" Perhaps my contact really was lying, but it's much more likely that I misunderstood what was said, or that someone misunderstood what was asked. Because trust between client and consultant is so important, I don't want to mistrust anyone unless I'm very sure of my grounds. I may decide that the particular client's ability to give information is not reliable, but that's entirely different from mistrusting someone's honesty.

HONESTY AND THE SEVENTH LAW OF TRUST

One of the most difficult traps for a consultant is the situation in which the client asks you to do something dishonest. Some years ago, a manager named Tim asked me to prepare a censored version of my checkup report that would be presented to the employees as the full report. I replied that it was my job to give him a full, honest report, and his job to distribute whatever parts of that report he saw fit. Tim agreed in principle, but asked if I would do him the favor of preparing the edited report, explaining that otherwise, he was afraid the true report would be leaked by the typing pool. That request seemed innocent enough, but I again refused.

Tim was so angry with me that I was sure I'd never get any future business. A year later, though, he called me to do another checkup. I decided to face the issue squarely and reminded him that he had been angry with me the last time we met.

"Yes, I was really burned," Tim confessed. "We had paid you a lot of money, and you wouldn't do me a tiny administrative favor. I was so angry I didn't really hear what you were saying until after you'd left. When I calmed down, I realized you were right."

One of the great advantages of not lying to your clients is that you generally don't have to remember what you said. This time, though, I wished I could remember. "I'm embarrassed to tell you this, but I don't really remember what I said."

Tim laughed. "I guess it was more important to me than to you. You told me that you were in the business of producing information, not packaging it. You said you would soon get confused if you started issuing multiple reports on the same information."

"I remember now," I said. "I offered to refund part of my fee to pay for having the report done outside your office."

"Yes, and that really ticked me off—at first. After a while, though, I realized that you were giving me a chance to see something important about my own organization and about myself. If I couldn't trust my own clerical staff with confidential reports, the problem was a lot bigger than this one report. I took a good look at myself and realized that I was being a bit paranoid."

The moral of this story stuck with me as The Seventh Law of Trust:

Never be dishonest, even if the client requests it.

If you turn down such a request, the client may remember you as uncooperative. But if you give in to a request for dishonesty, you'll always be remembered as a cheat. There's no better way to lose trust than to show you can only be trusted when nothing important is at stake.

PROMISES, PROMISES, AND TWO MORE LAWS OF TRUST

If your image as a cheat doesn't bother your client, you're still in trouble. Having done one dishonest service, you'll be expected to perform another the next time it's required. This principle applies just as well to perfectly honest acts: A service once given is a service promised for the future. Janice, the training director for one of my clients, once begged me to take twenty-two people into a workshop with a limit of twenty. I yielded when she pleaded that she simply didn't know how to handle the problem of turning them away, but I very carefully explained to her that this was a one-time, special favor.

In the next workshop, Janice again registered two extra people. When I argued that I wouldn't accept them, she said she thought it would be all right because I had allowed two extras in the previous group. She didn't remember my words, only my actions, which she took as implicit, blanket permission. If I now broke this implied promise, I would seem unreliable.

Experiences like this taught me, "Never promise anything you're not sure you can deliver." But nobody can be sure of the future, so an even better rule is The Eighth Law of Trust:

Never promise anything.

But how can a consultant succeed without ever making promises? Isn't every contract a promise? Yes, a contract is a promise, but a *contingent* promise. A contract says that I'll try to do something, and that if I do, you'll pay me so much for the service. If I don't succeed, you don't pay. A contract is also a *written* promise, which helps prevent you from unwittingly making implied promises.

But even the most tightly written contracts imply promises, so you can't really obey this rule. To compensate for its weakness, it must be accompanied by The Ninth Law of Trust:

Always keep your promise.

In Janice's case, I carefully explained to her that the workshop was noticeably poorer with twenty-two people, but she insisted that this alternative was better than her turning away two people at the last minute. Because we had an informal contract, I felt obligated to take the overflow to keep my promise. Since I already knew that words to Janice wouldn't change the informal contract, I changed our formal contract before the next workshop. I set a price of two thousand dollars a head for extra people. Janice accepted that as fair, and in subsequent workshops never needed another extra place.

CONTRACTS AND THE TENTH LAW OF TRUST

The subject of contracts brings me back to Jack. Jack once told me that he took a course on contracts in which the professor said there were only three very important rules to remember:

First, get it in writing.
Second, get it in writing.
Third, get it in writing.

I believe that every consultant should memorize these rules. Jack did, but there is more to the matter than Jack understood.

By all means get it in writing, but don't ever believe that a written contract will remove the need for trust between you and your client. A written contract is a useful way to prevent misunderstandings. All agreements involving money, for example, should definitely be written down somewhere and signed by both parties. But once trust goes, the written contract is worthless, so by all means follow The Tenth Law of Trust:

Get it in writing, but depend on trust.

To a consultant, trust without a contract is infinitely better than a contract without trust, in spite of anything Jack learned in school.

TRUST AND THE GOLDEN RULE

It makes a tidy package to have exactly ten laws, like the Ten Commandments. Still, it does seem an unlikely coincidence that all aspects of this important subject can be covered in just ten laws. Although the Ten Commandments went a long way, they did eventually have to be amended—which led to the founding of Christianity.

So, it's probably good to leave open the possibility of another law, one that covered all the cases that the others didn't anticipate, like the Eleventh Commandment. . . . What was that Eleventh Commandment anyway? It always slips my mind. But I do recall it covered the situations not handled by the first ten.

Perhaps if I could remember that Eleventh Commandment, I would know how to construct a final law of trust. I'll have to look it up some day. A rule like that would sure be Golden.

14

getting people to follow your advice

In spite of your best efforts, some plants will die
—Lessons from the Farm

How old is the profession of consulting? Some would argue that the serpent in the Garden of Eden was the first consultant, advising Eve (correctly) that God would surely not kill her for eating the forbidden fruit. Of course, the serpent neglected to warn her of the side effects, but no consultant is perfect. That's why consultants need advice themselves. So, in this final chapter, I share with you advice from one of my own consultants.

ROOTS

Traveling is fun, but after a few weeks toiling in the fleshpots of the world, it's nice to have a place where I have roots. Like Voltaire's Candide, I like to come home to my tiny farm and cultivate my garden.

One of the benefits of living on a farm is getting to know farmers. For city folks, getting to know farmers is a rather slow process, because farms operate on a different time scale. You might live next door to a farmer—that is, half a mile away—for a couple of years before you start exchanging more than a single word at a time. You might wave when passing, or say "hello" if you're close enough, but it takes a few seasons before you graduate to advanced topics. Like whether it's going to rain in the next few days. Or when the first frost is likely.

On the other hand, if there's a natural disaster, such as a blizzard, ice-storm, or flood, your neighbors will suddenly appear with all sorts of equipment, food, and help of every imaginable kind. Not a lot of words—just help. On the other hand, if you don't want the help, just a nod of the head and a "thanks" and they'll disappear back into silence.

Because farmers don't talk much, some city folks think that farmers are simple-minded. Nothing could be further from the truth. Every one of my neighbors is involved in a multimillion-dollar business that is intricately interconnected with twenty other businesses. For example, we have a few acres that we can't farm usefully so we have a barter arrangement with John, our neighbor who runs a dairy farm. He plants grass or grain on our property, which keeps the soil in good condition. In addition, he gives us all the straw and manure we want for our garden, and does various odd jobs now and then around our place. This barter is part of an intricate trade network. It balances off over the years so that everything comes out even, although no money changes hands.

When the manure is delivered we get another benefit, because John looks at our garden. He'll never give us any advice unless we ask, but over the years we've learned to ask. Last spring, I was planting corn when John drove over with some manure. He stood in utter silence, watching me pack the corn seed into the ground. He didn't say a word, but I got the feeling from his expression that maybe I ought to ask.

"Do you have any corn this year?" I said as a way of breaking the ice.

"Yep," he said, "Is that what you're planting?"

"Sure, don't you recognize it?"

"Oh, I didn't recognize the way you're planting it. We don't plant corn quite like that. What system are you using?"

"Well," I said, a little defensively, "I heard that you had to pack the corn seed down into the ground so that the plants would be firmly rooted."

"Is that so?"

"Sure," I said. "You yourself told me that it was important for the corn to be well-rooted so it wouldn't get blown down in a windstorm."

"Well, yes, I did tell you that. But I didn't tell you to press them down into the ground."

"But right here on the packet it says, 'Push firmly into the ground.'"

"Of course," he said. "That's to keep the seeds from washing away if we get a heavy rain. But you're grinding them down with your heel. All you're doing is packing the soil so hard that the roots won't be able to develop properly. You want that soil to be nice and loose where the roots are going to come out. Pressing on it just won't do any good at all."

After John left, I changed my planting tactics in mid-row. That summer, I watched those corn plants grow. It might have been my imagination, but the ones I packed down with my heel didn't do so well. They germinated poorly, and the ones that did survive never looked as healthy as the others.

A few months later, John was back again delivering some straw for mulching the garden. We got into a discussion about my watering habits, and it followed pretty much the same track as before. After a long time, I finally coaxed out of him the information that I was overwatering the corn. I explained that I was trying to give them a lot of water so that they would develop a strong root system.

John chuckled a little and pointed out to me that a little dryness now and again forced the plant to extend its roots further down into the ground in search of moisture. This made the roots deeper and therefore stronger, which gave the plant a much better chance of surviving when the winds were blowing. If, for some reason, I didn't get around to watering them, they'd be able to take care of themselves.

None of this was in the form of telling me that that was the right way to do it. He just kind of pointed out some of the principles to me and then kept quiet and went on his way. Later, when some of the plants died anyway, he just shrugged his shoulders and said, "That's why you plant extras."

After ten years of this kind of gentle advice, I've become a passably good gardener. At least, I'm getting three to four times as much produce from the same amount of land, with about one-third the labor.

LESSONS FROM THE FARM

It struck me the other day when I was trying to make a list of consultants that John is my gardening consultant. I hadn't realized this for ten years, which makes John the perfect consultant. His style is derived from the whole farming approach, which itself is derived from a long life of observing plants and the way they respond to different kinds of treatment. I made a list of some of the things he's taught me about gardening and, looking at the list, I realized that it would be an excellent list to give someone who wanted to know how to get his advice followed with any kind of client. Here are some of the things John taught me:

1. *Never use cheap seed.* Seeds are like ideas. By the time you're finished raising a plant, the cost of the seed is a very small part of the whole farming operation. And the cost of getting an idea is very small compared with the amount you're going to invest in trying to make that idea develop. So, make sure that your ideas are of the best quality. Do whatever you can to get the best ideas before you invest a lot of money cultivating them.

2. *A prepared soil is the secret of all gardening.* We tend to look at what grows above ground, but most of what a plant is doing is out of our sight. Even the best seed won't grow in poorly prepared soil. Good soil takes years to prepare, but with good seed and good soil, almost nothing you do can make it go wrong. In fact, it's best if you just leave it alone and let the soil do the work. In other words, it's the preparation before you plant an idea that makes most of the difference as to whether it works or not.

3. *Timing is critical.* The best seed planted too early will be killed off as a tiny sprout by an untimely frost. The best seed planted too late will never quite reach maturity and bear fruit. Farmers spend a lot of time looking at the sky, feeling the soil, doing whatever is necessary to figure out just what's the right time to plant their seeds. Too often, consultants broadcast their ideas the moment they happen to get them, rather than the moment that's right for germination.

4. *The plants that hold firmest are the ones that develop their own roots.* You don't get strong roots on a plant by packing the dirt around them so that the plant will hold firmly in the soil. You just prepare the soil, put the seed in there and let it hold on for itself. You might have to protect it a little bit when it's small but the less protection you give it, the hardier the plant is going to be. The same is true for ideas, but sometimes we can't seem to resist grinding them into the ground.

5. *Excessive watering produces weakness, not strength.* Too much water weakens a plant because it doesn't need to put its roots down deep into the earth. The same is true of too much fertilizer. If too much fertilizer is given a plant, it will produce all leaves and no fruit. We all want to get support for our ideas, which sometimes leads us into overselling. Too many resources poured into a young idea produces lots of action, but few results. Ideas, like plants, thrive on a certain amount of struggle.

6. *In spite of your best efforts, some plants will die.* If you plan a garden around the idea that every plant must be a prize winner, you'll always be disappointed. If you count on all plants to live, you may go hungry. Farmers, because they're always working with a large, complex system, learn to live with failure and to not take it personally.

Well, those are some of the secrets I've gotten from *my* consultant. I considered casting them into laws, but I don't think John would like that. Laws are not his style, and he might have been tempted to observe that perhaps consultants love their ideas too much, or don't realize how small they are, when compared with the real problems. I want to think about that for a while, but for now, I'll just have to cultivate my garden.

Readings and Other Experiences:
Where to Go If You Want More

One book does not a consultant make. I've been consulting for more than thirty years, I've read thousands of books, and yet I still keep learning more and more every year. Even so, it's easy for me to fall into the trap of believing that I *finally* know everything worth knowing, and that all I have to do is go forth and spread my knowledge in the world. That's why I believe that every consultant should create and follow a personal learning program.

My own program includes a minimum of one book a month and one major workshop a year. Whenever possible, of course, I manage more, and try especially to learn through my work. That's the best way, but not the only way. I also use my clients as sources of good ideas for where to learn. Most new books I read and workshops I attend result from clients' suggestions. It stands to reason that clients ask *me* for suggestions in return, so the pages that follow are some ideas that might get you learning even more secrets of consulting.

EFFECTIVE THINKING

Several decades ago, I did my graduate research on thinking and problem-solving, topics that were then on the far fringes of psychology. In the past few years, however, thinking and problem-solving have finally begun to be recognized as legitimate topics, and some terrific books have emerged. One of the earliest good ones is

Adams, James L. *Conceptual Blockbusting*. San Francisco: W.H. Freeman, 1974.

Adams deals with the subject of how to get unstuck, a perfect book for jigglers of all sorts.

Another one of the early classics is

McKim, Robert H. *Experiences in Visual Thinking*, 2nd ed. Monterey, Calif.: Brooks/Cole, 1980.

211

McKim trains the mind to think in terms of visual images, to counteract the human tendency to get stuck in verbal traps.

A much broader approach is found in

Waddington, C.H. *Tools for Thought*. New York: Basic Books, 1977.

Waddington surveys a great variety of thinking tools and aids, some formal, some informal, some new, some old.

Of course, many of these tools are "new" only because of our ignorance of the past. I have been particularly delighted and influenced by the works of the Sufis, who have studied and taught how to jiggle for many centuries. Sufis, among other things, are masters of the paradoxical methods. If you don't know Sufi literature, you might start with the most amusing and enlightening:

Shah, Idries. *Wisdom of the Idiots*. London: Octagon Press, 1969.

Although this source is excellent, you could start with almost any book by Idries Shah, who has almost single-handedly brought Sufi thought to the modern Western reader.

My publishers and my accountant would be quite upset if I didn't refer you to some of my own work on problem-solving. An easy and friendly book is

Gause, Donald C., and Gerald M. Weinberg. *Are Your Lights On?: How to Figure Out What the Problem Really Is*. Boston: Little, Brown, 1982.

If you intend to make your living solving problems, it's particularly important to be sure you're working on the right problem. Good problem definition helps you get started right, and starting right is especially important for consultants. About twenty-five years ago, I decided to write a book about what goes through my head in the first five minutes of approaching a new situation, and particularly about the effort to encompass the entire situation. After fifteen years, the project has grown to at least four planned volumes, the first two of which are

Weinberg, Gerald M. *An Introduction to General Systems Thinking*. New York: Wiley-Interscience, 1975.

_____ , and Daniela Weinberg. *On the Design of Stable Systems.* New York: Wiley-Interscience, 1981.

These are tougher reading than the volume in hand, but many consultants have told me that the benefit repaid the effort. At first glance, they may look mathematical, but they're actually intended to demystify subjects that have previously been hidden in mathematical guises.

WORKING WITH PEOPLE

All consultants work with people, so no matter how technical your consulting practice, you will surely benefit from improving your ability to work with others. For fifty years, the guaranteed starting place for this self-improvement task has been

Carnegie, Dale. *How to Win Friends and Influence People.* New York: Simon and Schuster, 1936.

It's been revised and modernized, but the essentials are the same as they have been for two generations now.

Another, more recent, but equally down-to-earth book is

Bolton, Robert. *People Skills: How to Assert Yourself, Listen to Others, and Resolve Conflicts.* Englewood Cliffs, N.J.: Prentice-Hall, 1979.

No matter how skilled and experienced you are as a consultant, you can probably benefit from Bolton's systematic review of "people skills." I did.

COUNSELING

One very special set of skills is counseling people about personal problems. Consultants often find themselves in the role of counselors to their clients, sometimes drifting into this slippery role before they notice. That's why I recommend the following book to all professional consultants:

Kennedy, Eugene. *On Becoming a Counselor.* New York: Continuum Publishing Co., 1900.

Kennedy's book is directed to those who are not professional counselors, but who frequently find themselves in this role and at least want to know how to avoid doing harm.

MEETINGS

Another role quite familiar to consultants is participant in or facilitator of meetings. The time that consultants spend in meetings would be more useful if they had studied

> Doyle, Michael, and David Straus. *How to Make Meetings Work*. Chicago: Playboy Press, 1976.

Doyle and Straus have developed the "interaction method" for organizing and operating meetings of all types. Using this method, clearly described in this book, I've helped dozens of my clients to convert their meetings from the worst of times to the best of times.

There are other good books on meetings, but *How to Make Meetings Work* is my favorite—except for the following book on specialized technical meetings:

> Freedman, Daniel P., and Gerald M. Weinberg. *Handbook of Walkthroughs, Inspections, and Technical Reviews*, 3rd ed. Boston: Little, Brown, 1982.

Much of my consulting takes the form of critical reviews of work in progress. Technical reviews can be a source of technical growth, or great anxiety and conflict, depending on how they are led. I feel that the *Handbook*, with its question-and-answer format, is an essential guide for all people who spend time in review meetings. But, of course, I'm prejudiced.

HANDLING RESISTANCE

I've already written that my approach to handling resistance starts from the work of

> Block, Peter. *Flawless Consulting: A Guide to Getting Your Expertise Used*. San Diego: University Associates, 1981.

This book is of great interest to consultants generally, but it's especially good on the subjects of resistance and of setting the right "contract" with clients.

A more specialized book entirely on the subject of resistance is

Anderson, Carol M., and Susan Stewart. *Mastering Resistance.*
New York: The Guilford Press, 1983.

Anderson and Stewart write from the perspective of family therapists, but if you skip the historical and theoretical parts, the rest should be most useful to almost any consultant.

THE FAMILY MODEL

The family model is a powerful one for almost any consulting situation, an insight that has been especially propagated by Virginia Satir, as in

Satir, Virginia. *Conjoint Family Therapy*, 3rd ed. Palo Alto, Calif.: Science and Behavior Books, 1983.

and

_____ . *Peoplemaking.* Palo Alto, Calif.: Science and Behavior Books, 1972.

I have been greatly influenced by the work of Virginia Satir. I first became aware of her radical approach through my reading of *Peoplemaking*, which provides a good survey of her approach to relearning to interact with others. *Conjoint Family Therapy* is more of a comprehensive textbook aimed at family therapists, but like all her books, it is written without academic pretension.

Much more powerful than her books are her workshops, which range from one day to one month in length. They are attended by consultants in many fields, including those outside family therapy; I wholeheartedly recommend them to all my readers.

LABORATORY TRAINING

There are many other groups that offer experiential training of value to those who wish to influence others. Experiential (or laboratory) training seems more expensive than other forms of training, but when it's good, it's worth much more. It's important, though, to be sure that you're choosing a top-notch trainer, and the best way to do that is through personal reference.

I can personally vouch for training offered through the Avanta Network, organized by Virginia Satir:

Avanta Network
139 Forest Avenue
Palo Alto, CA 94301

I have also had many remarkable learning experiences through the NTL Institute:

NTL Institute
P.O. Box 9155
Rosslyn Station
Arlington, VA 22209

Of course, I personally recommend the workshops that Dani and I offer and that you can learn about by writing to

Weinberg and Weinberg
Rural Route Two
Lincoln, NE 68520

TRUST

Naturally, you can trust me on the Weinberg and Weinberg workshops, but you ought to cut the cards. The only book I know that's devoted to the crucial topic of trust is

Gibb, Jack R. *Trust: A New View of Personal and Organizational Development.* Los Angeles: The Guild of Tutors Press, 1978.

It's worth reading.

THE CONSULTING TRADE

There are a number of books written about consulting by consultants. Block's *Flawless Consulting* is, in my opinion, the best, followed by

Steele, Fritz. *Consulting for Organizational Change.* Amherst, Mass.: University of Massachusetts Press, 1975.

Both Block and Steele are concerned with depth rather than breadth, their books covering the most important and difficult topics rather than all possible topics. Still, I suppose we must have books that attempt to cover everything, and one of those is

> Lippitt, Gordon, and Ronald Lippitt. *The Consulting Process in Action*. La Jolla, Calif.: University Associates, 1978.

Although I learned a great deal from Ron Lippitt many years ago when he was my teacher, I didn't seem to learn much from this book, perhaps because of the attempt to be too broad. Or perhaps it was the lack of the personal touch.

Even so, there are people who prefer a more academic approach, at least on certain subjects. Those people might like

> Nadler, David. *Feedback and Organizational Development: Using Data-Based Methods*. Reading, Mass.: Addison-Wesley, 1977.

Nadler writes about gathering data in organizations. Personally, I prefer more of a participant-observer approach to these "data-based" methods, but consultants must develop their own styles to suit their personalities and skills.

THE CONSULTING BUSINESS

Even less personal are several books that attempt to survey consulting as a business. For example,

> Greiner, Larry E., and Robert Metzger. *Consulting to Management*. Englewood Cliffs, N.J.: Prentice-Hall, 1983.

and

> Kelley, Robert E. *Consulting: The Complete Guide to a Profitable Career*. New York: Charles Scribner's Sons, 1981.

My first reaction when I read books like these is that if you need them to succeed as a consultant, you probably won't succeed as a consultant. On the other hand, I know that some otherwise excellent consultants fail because they don't take care of certain nuts-and-bolts details, like sending out bills and keeping tax records. These books do give people an overview of what is required to be a professional, especially the nuts-and-bolts we'd rather not think of.

PERSONAL DEVELOPMENT

The Journal

In the final analysis, the self is the primary tool of all consultants. There are so many possible paths to self-development, but I argue that one essential tool for self-development is the personal journal. The journal does many things for you that your own personal consultant does. Without a journal, it's hard to get a perspective on yourself over time. Ira Progoff is the acknowledged leader of the current journal movement, and you might want to read

> Progoff, Ira. *At a Journal Workshop.* New York: Dialogue House Library, 1975.

I think keeping a journal is so valuable that I devote a chapter to the technique in a book to be published next year:

> Weinberg, Gerald M. *Becoming a Technical Leader.* New York: Dorset House Publishing Co., 1986.

On the other hand, you don't need a book to start a journal. Just buy yourself a bound notebook and start writing down your thoughts and observations about yourself.

Continuing Education

Because of their irregular schedule, consultants may have difficulty using conventional systems of education. More than other people, they have to take responsibility for their own learning. That's why every consultant should have a look at

> Gross, Ronald. *The Lifelong Learner.* New York: Simon and Schuster, 1979.

It's full of ideas, suggestions, and specific resources for self-renewal, most of which can be accomplished on a consultant's schedule and budget.

Happiness

My final suggestions concern books that fall into no particular category other than they can help you in becoming a better person. Several authors have influenced me greatly, and I would like to share them with you. We can start with Virginia Satir, whom I've already mentioned, and three short books of hers that anybody can read with great personal benefit:

> Satir, Virginia. *Self-Esteem.* Milbrae, Calif.: Celestial Arts, 1975.

_____ . *Making Contact*. Milbrae, Calif.: Celestial Arts, 1976.

_____ . *Your Many Faces*. Milbrae, Calif.: Celestial Arts, 1978.

Virginia Satir was greatly influenced by Carl Rogers, and so was I. If you don't know Rogers, you may want to read one or more of his books:

Rogers, Carl. *On Personal Power*. New York: Dell, 1977.

_____ . *On Becoming a Person*. Boston: Houghton Mifflin, 1961.

_____ . *A Way of Being*. Boston: Houghton Mifflin, 1980.

Finally, I must mention Bertrand Russell. Although his Nobel Prize for literature was probably not much influenced by this little book, *I* was influenced by it:

Russell, Bertrand. *The Conquest of Happiness*. New York: Signet Books, 1951.

In his usual direct manner, Russell tackles the ancient question of how to be happy, and succeeds. It's hard to imagine a better example of effective consulting.

Listing of Laws, Rules, and Principles

The Bolden Rule: If you can't fix it, feature it. (p. 43)

Boulding's Backward Basis: Things are the way they are because they got that way. (p. 58)

Brown's Brilliant Bequest: Words are often useful, but it always pays to listen to the music (especially your own internal music). (p. 85)

The Buffalo Bridle: You can make buffalo go anywhere just so long as they want to go there. (p. 160)

Charlotte's Law: Market for quality, not quantity. (p. 179)

The Credit Rule: You'll never accomplish anything if you care who gets the credit. (p. 8)

The Dealer's Choice: Let them try whatever they like, but teach them how to protect themselves. (p. 143) Always trust your client—and cut the cards. (p. 200)

The Duncan Hines Difference: It tastes better when you add your own egg. (p. 177)

The Edsel Edict: If you must have something new, take one, not two. (p. 145)

The Eighth Law of Marketing: It tastes better when you add your own egg. (p. 177)

The Eighth Law of Pricing: Price is not a thing, it's a negotiated relationship. (p. 189)

The Eighth Law of Trust: Never promise anything. (p. 203)

The Fast-Food Fallacy: No difference plus no difference plus no difference plus . . . eventually equals a clear difference. (p. 131)

The Fifth Law of Marketing: Never let a single client have more than one-fourth of your business. (p. 173)

The Fifth Law of Pricing: If you need the money, don't take the job. (p. 187)

The Fifth Law of Trust: People are never liars—in their own eyes. (p. 200)

The First Law of Consulting: In spite of what your client may tell you, there's always a problem. (p. 5)

The First Law of Engineering: If it ain't broke, don't fix it. (p. 39)

The First Law of Marketing: A consultant can exist in one of two states: State I (idle) or State B (busy). (p. 170)

The First Law of Pricing: Pricing has many functions, only one of which is the exchange of money. (p. 184)

The First Law of Trust: Nobody but you cares about the reason you let them down. (p. 196)

Fisher's Fundamental Theorem: The better adapted you are, the less adaptable you tend to be. (p. 30)

The Five-Minute Rule: Clients always know how to solve their problems, and always tell the solution in the first five minutes. (p. 67)

Ford's Fundamental Feedback Formula: People can take any amount of water from any stream to use for any purpose desired. People must return an equal amount of water *upstream* from the point from which they took it. (p. 133)

The Fourth Law of Consulting: If they didn't hire you, don't solve their problem. (p. 9)

The Fourth Law of Marketing: Clients are more important to you than you can ever be to them. (p. 172)

The Fourth Law of Pricing: Pricing is not a zero-sum game. (p. 186)

The Fourth Law of Trust: The trick of earning trust is to avoid all tricks. (p. 198)

The Gilded Rule: If you can't feature it, fake it. (p. 48)

Halstead's variation: The biggest and longest lasting changes usually originate in attempts to preserve the very thing that ultimately changes most. (p. 132)

The Harder Law: Once you eliminate your number one problem, YOU promote number two. (p. 17)

The Hardest Law: Helping myself is even harder than helping others. (p. 18)

The Hard Law: If you can't accept failure, you'll never succeed as a consultant. (p. 16)

The Hard Law, Inverted: Some people do succeed as consultants, so it must be possible to deal with failure. (p. 16)

Homer's Rule: Struggling to travel can make you a stay-at-home. (p. 128)

The Incongruence Insight: When words and music don't go together, they point to a missing element. (p. 84)

The Inverse Gilded Rule: If something's faked, it must need fixing. (p. 49)

The Label Law: Most of us buy the label, not the merchandise. (p. 64) The name of the thing is not the thing. (p. 64)

The Law of Raspberry Jam: The wider you spread it, the thinner it gets. (p. 11) Influence or affluence; take your choice. (p. 11)

The Law of the Hammer: The child who receives a hammer for Christmas will discover that everything needs pounding. (p. 53)

The Law of the Jiggle: Less is more. (p. 113)

Lessons from the Farm: Never use cheap seed. (p. 209) A prepared soil is the secret of all gardening. (p. 209) Timing is critical. (p. 209) The plants that hold firmest are the ones that develop their own roots. (p. 210) Excessive watering produces weakness, not strength. (p. 210) In spite of your best efforts, some plants will die. (p. 210)

The Level Law: Effective problem-solvers may have many problems, but rarely have a single, dominant problem. (p. 72)

The Lone Ranger Fantasy: When the clients don't show their appreciation, pretend that they're stunned by your performance—but never forget that it's your fantasy, not theirs. (p. 8)

Lynne's Law of Life: To be able to say yes to yourself as a consultant, be able to say no to any of your clients. (p. 174)

The Main Maxim: What you don't know may not hurt you, but what you don't remember always does. (p. 92)

Marvin's Fifth Great Secret: Make sure they pay you enough so they'll do what you say. (p. 41) The most important act in consulting is setting the right fee. (p. 41)

Marvin's First Great Secret: Ninety percent of all illness cures itself—with absolutely no intervention from the doctor. (p. 38) Deal gently with systems that should be able to cure themselves. (p. 39)

Marvin's Fourth Great Secret: Whatever the client is doing, advise something else. (p. 7) If what they've been doing hasn't solved the problem, tell them to do something else. (p. 41)

Marvin's Second Great Secret: Repeatedly curing a system that can cure itself will eventually create a system that can't. (p. 40)

Marvin's Sixth Great Secret: Know-how pays much less than know-when. (p. 42)

Marvin's Third Great Secret: Every prescription has two parts: the medicine and the method of ensuring correct use. (p. 40)

The New Law: Nothing new ever works. (p. 141)

The Ninth Law of Marketing: Spend at least one-fourth of your time doing nothing. (p. 177)

The Ninth Law of Pricing: Set the price so you won't regret it either way. (p. 190); see also *The Principle of Least Regret.*

The Ninth Law of Trust: Always keep your promise. (p. 203)

The Number One Secret: Consulting ain't as easy as it looks. (p. 3)

The Orange Juice Test: "We can do it—and this is how much it will cost." (p. 33)

Pandora's Pox: Nothing new ever works, but there's always hope that this time will be different. (p. 142)

The Potato Chip Principle: If you know your audience, it's easy to set triggers. (p. 93)

Prescott's Pickle Principle: Cucumbers get more pickled than brine gets cucumbered. (p. 125) A small system that tries to change a big system through long and continued contact is more likely to be changed itself. (p. 125)

The Principle of Least Regret: Set the price so you won't regret it either way. (p. 190); see also *The Ninth Law of Pricing.*

Rhonda's First Revelation: It may look like a crisis, but it's only the end of an illusion. (p. 149)

Rhonda's Second Revelation: When change is inevitable, we struggle most to keep what we value most. (p. 150)

Rhonda's Third Revelation: When you create an illusion, to prevent or soften change, the change becomes more likely—and harder to take. (p. 151)

Roamer's Rule: Struggling to stay at home can make you a wanderer. (p. 127)

Romer's Rule: The best way to lose something is to struggle to keep it. (p. 128)

Rudy's Rutabaga Rule: Once you eliminate your number one problem, number two gets a promotion. (p. 15)

The Rule of Three: If you can't think of three things that might go wrong with your plans, then there's something wrong with your thinking. (p. 81)

The Second Law of Consulting: No matter how it looks at first, it's always a people problem. (p. 5)

The Second Law of Marketing: The best way to get clients is to have clients. (p. 170)

The Second Law of Pricing: The more they pay you, the more they love you. (p. 184) The less they pay you, the less they respect you. (p. 184)

The Second Law of Trust: Trust takes years to win, moments to lose. (p. 197)

The Seventh Law of Marketing: Give away your best ideas. (p. 176)

The Seventh Law of Pricing: Money is more than price. (p. 188)

The Seventh Law of Trust: Never be dishonest, even if the client requests it. (p. 202)

The Sixth Law of Marketing: The best marketing tool is a satisfied client. (p. 170)

The Sixth Law of Pricing: If they don't like your work, don't take their money. (p. 188)

The Sixth Law of Trust: Always trust your client—and cut the cards. (p. 200)

Sparks's Law of Problem Solution: The chances of solving a problem decline the closer you get to finding out who was the cause of the problem. (p. 58)

Study guides: Keep it simple and not too detailed; you're a consultant, not a district attorney. (p. 58) Study for understanding, not for criticism. (p. 59) Look for what you like in the present situation, and comment on it. (p. 59)

The Ten Percent Promise Law: Never promise more than ten percent improvement. (p. 6)

The Ten Percent Solution Law: If you happen to achieve more than ten percent improvement, make sure it isn't noticed. (p. 6)

The Tenth Law of Marketing: Market for quality, not quantity. (p. 179)

The Tenth Law of Pricing: All prices are ultimately based on feelings, both yours and theirs. (p. 191)

The Tenth Law of Trust: Get it in writing, but depend on trust. (p. 204)

The Third Law of Consulting: Never forget they're paying you by the hour, not by the solution. (p. 5)

The Third Law of Marketing: Spend at least one day a week getting exposure. (p. 171)

The Third Law of Pricing: The money is usually the smallest part of the price. (p. 185)

The Third Law of Trust: People don't tell you when they stop trusting you. (p. 197)

The Third-Time Charm: Consultants tend to be the most effective on the third problem you give them. (p. 32)

The Three-Finger Rule: When you point a finger at someone, notice where the other three fingers are pointing. (p. 66)

The Time Bomb: Time wounds all heels. (p. 147) The surest way to waste time is to throw caution to the winds. (p. 147)

The Titanic Effect: The thought that disaster is impossible often leads to an unthinkable disaster. (p. 95)

The Tradeoff Treatment: You don't get nothin' for nothin'. (p. 24) Moving in one direction incurs a cost in the other. (p. 27)

The Volkswagen Verity: If you can't refuse it, defuse it. (p. 146)

Weinberg's Law of Fetch: Sometimes farfetched is only shortsighted. (p. 80)

Weinbergs' Law of Twins: Most of the time, for most of the world, no matter how hard people work at it, nothing of any significance happens. (p. 13)

Weinbergs' Law of Twins, Inverted: Some of the time, in some places, significant change happens—especially when people aren't working hard at it. (p. 123)

The Weinberg Test: Would you place your own life in the hands of this system? (p. 135)

The White Bread Warning: If you use the same recipe, you get the same bread. (p. 56)

The Why Whammy: We may run out of energy, or air, or water, or food, but we'll never run out of reasons. (p. 62)

Index